Government Intervention in the Canadian Nuclear Industry

G. Bruce Doern

The Institute for Research on Public Policy
L'Institut de recherches politiques

Montreal
1980

© The Institute for Research on Public Policy   1980
   All rights reserved

ISBN 0-920380-46-8

Legal Deposit First Quarter
Bibliothèque nationale du Québec

Institute for Research on Public Policy/Institut de recherches politiques
2149 MacKay
Montréal, Québec H3G 2J2

*Typesetting by Judy Bradley assisted by
Cheryl MacDougall-Wilkie*

Printing by Tri-Graphic Printing (Ottawa) Ltd.

Founded in 1972, the INSTITUTE FOR RESEARCH ON PUBLIC POLICY is a national organization whose independence and autonomy are ensured by the revenues of an endowment fund which is supported by the federal and provincial governments and by the private sector. In addition, the institute receives grants and contracts from governments, corporations, and foundations to carry out specific research projects.

The *raison d'être* of the institute is threefold:

— To act as a catalyst within the national community by helping to facilitate informed public debate on issues of major public interest

— To stimulate participation by all segments of the national community in the process that leads to public policy making

— To find practical solutions to important public policy problems, thus aiding in the development of sound public policies.

The institute is governed by a Board of Directors, which is its decision-making body, and a Council of Trustees, which advises the board on matters related to the research direction of the institute. Day to day administration of the institute's policies, programmes, and staff is the responsibility of the president.

The institute operates in a decentralized way, employing researchers located across Canada. This ensures that research undertaken will include contributions from all regions of the country.

Wherever possible, the institute will try to promote public understanding of, and discussion on, issues of national importance, whether they be controversial or not. The institute will publish its research findings with clarity and impartiality. It is not the function of the institute to control or influence the conduct of particular research or the conclusions reached thereby. Conclusions or recommendations in IRPP publications are solely those of the author, and should not be attributed to the Board of Directors, Council of Trustees, or contributors to the institute.

The president bears final responsibility for the decision to publish a manuscript under an IRPP imprint. In reaching this decision, he is advised on the accuracy and objectivity of a manuscript by both internal IRPP staff and outside reviewers. Publication of a manuscript signifies that it is deemed to be a competent treatment of a subject worthy of public consideration.

Publications of the institute are published in the language of the author, along with an executive summary in both of Canada's official languages.

THE MEMBERS OF THE INSTITUTE

Board of Directors

The Honourable John B. Aird, Q.C.
  (Chairman)
  Aird & Berlis, Toronto
James Black
  President, The Molson Companies
  Limited, Toronto
Claude Castonguay
  President, The Laurentian Fund Inc.
Guy Chabot
  Raymond, Chabot, Martin & Paré,
  Montreal
Dr. Garl C.A. Cook
  Senior Advisor on the Regulation
  Reference to the Chairman of the
  Economic Council
James S. Cowan
  Stewart, MacKeen & Covert, Halifax
Dr. H.E. Duckworth
  President, Uniersity of Winnipeg
Dr. James Fleck
  Faculty of Management Studies, University
  of Toronto
Dr. Reva Gerstein
  Consultant, Toronto
Hon. William Hamilton
  President & Chief Executive Officer,
  Employers' Council of British Columbia
Tom Kent
  Dean of Administrative Studies,
  Dalhousie University
Dr. Michael J.L. Kirby
  President, IRPP
Hon. Donald Macdonald
  McCarthy & McCarthy, Toronto
Gerald A.B. McGavin
  President, Yorkshire Trust, Vancouver
E.M. Mills
  Associate Director, Banff Centre, Banff
Pierre O'Neil
  Director, Television News, Radio-Canada,
  Montreal
James F. O'Sullivan
  Vice-President, Finance & Administration,
  University of New Brunswick,
  Fredericton
Hon. Robert Stanfield
  Former Leader, Progressive Conservative
  Party of Canada
Eldon D. Thompson
  Saint John, N.B.
Bryan Vaughan
  Honorary Chairman, Vickers & Benson,
  Toronto

Secretary
Peter C. Dobell
  Parliamentary Centre, Ottawa

Treasurer
Dr. Louis G. Vagianos
  Vice-President, Dalhousie University,
  Halifax

Executive Committee
The Honourable John B. Aird (Chairman)
Eldon D. Thompson (Vice-Chairman)
Dr. Michael J.L. Kirby
E.M. Mills
Pierre O'Neil

Investment Committee
Hon. Donald Macdonald (Chairman)
Tom Kierans (Vice-Chairman)
Peter C. Dobell
Dr. Michael J.L. Kirby
Paul Little
  Vice-President, Finance
  All Pak Products Ltd.

Council of Trustees

Government Representatives
Fred Dickson, Nova Scotia
Harry Hobbs, Alberta
Darwin Kealey, Ontario
Don Leitch, Manitoba
Douglas T. Monroe, Yukon
Robert Normand, Quebec
John H. Parker, Northwest Territories
Gordon Robertson, Canada
Gordon Smith, Canada
Barry Toole, New Brunswick
David Vardy, Newfoundland
Murray Wallace, Saskatchewan
Andrew Wells, Prince Edward Island

Members at Large
Dr. Stefan Dupré (Chairman)
  Department of Political Economy,
  University of Toronto
Doris Anderson
  Chairman, Advisory Council on the Status
  of Women, Ottawa
Dr. Francis Bairstow
  Director, Industrial Relations Centre,
  McGill University, Montreal
Dr. Roger Blais
  Dean of Research, Ecole Polytechnique,
  Montreal
Robert W. Bonner, Q.C.
  Bonner & Fouks, Vancouver
Professor John L. Brown
  Faculty of Business Administration &
  Commerce, University of Alberta,
  Edmonton

Dr. Mark Eliesen
  Director, Federal NDP Caucus Research Bureau, Ottawa
W.A. Friley
  President, Skyland Oil, Calgary
Judge Nathan Green
  The Law Courts, Halifax
Donald S. Harvie
  Chairman, Devonian Foundation
Dr. Leon Katz
  Dept. of Physics, Univ. of Saskatchewan, Saskatoon
Tom Kierans
  Vice-Chairman, Pitfield, MacKay, Ross, Toronto
Dr. Leo Kristjanson
  Vice-President, Planning University of Saskatchewan
Andrée Lajoie
  Director, Centre for Research on Public Law, University of Montreal
Allen T. Lambert
  Chairman, Toronto-Dominion Bank, Toronto
Terry Mactaggart
  Executive Director, Niagara Institute, Niagara-on-the-Lake
Professor William A.W. Neilson
  Faculty of Law, University of Victoria
Marilyn L. Pilkington
  Tory, Tory, DesLauriers, Binnington, Toronto
Adélard Savoie, Q.C.
  Yeoman, Savoie, LeBlanc & DeWitt, Moncton
Philip Vineberg, Q.C.
  Phillips, Vineberg, Goodman, Phillips & Rothman, Montreal

Dr. Norman Wagner
  President, University of Calgary
Mrs. Ida Wasacase
  Director, Saskatchewan Indian Federated College, University of Regina
Prof. Paul Weiler
  Mackenzie King Professor, Harvard University
Dr. John Tuzo Wilson
  Director General, Ontario Science Centre, Toronto
Ray Wolfe
  President, The Oshawa Group, Toronto

Ex Officio Members
Dr. Owen Carrigan
  Representing the Canada Council
Denis Cole
  President, Institute of Public Administration of Canada
A.J. Earp
  President, Association of Universities & Colleges of Canada
Dr. Claude Fortier
  President, Science Council of Canada
Larkin Kerwin
  President, Royal Society of Canada
Dr. William G. Schneider
  President, National Research Council
Dr. René Simard
  President, Medical Research Council
Dr. David Slater
  Acting Chairman, Economic Council of Canada
Professor André Vachet
  Representing the Social Science Federation of Canada

Preface

In November 1977 the Institute launched its Regulation and Government Intervention Program. Since then we have published a dozen books exploring a number of aspects of government activity in Canada: competition policy, public employment and compensation, energy policy, regulation and public decision-making, regulation and federal-provincial relations, federal airline regulation, provincial regulation of occupational health and safety and decision-making about tariff and non-tariff barriers to trade.

In this volume Professor Doern looks at government intervention in Canada's nuclear industry. In particular, he examines the similarities and differences among three types of intervention: public ownership (for the production of power generating reactors); regulation (of the occupational health of uranium miners); and long term contracts (for uranium oxide for Ontario Hydro). While it answers some questions about the substitutability of certain instruments of public policy, this study raises others. For example, when we look very closely, what is it that distinguishes public ownership from long term contracts where the government buys virtually all of an industry's output? Are the differences more of semantics than of substance?

Nuclear policy is likely to be more important in the years ahead. This volume helps to understand the past so that we may face the future better prepared.

Michael J.L. Kirby
President
February, 1980

Préface

En novembre 1977, l'Institut lançait son Programme d'étude de la réglementation et de l'intervention gouvernementales. Nous avons publié depuis une douzaine d'ouvrages sur divers aspects de l'activité des gouvernements au Canada dans ces domaines: politique de concurrence, emploi et traitements dans le secteur public, politique énergétique, réglementation et processus décisionnel dans le secteur public, réglementation et relations fédérales-provinciales, réglementation fédérale des compagnies aériennes, réglementation provinciale de la santé et de la sécurité professionnelles, prise des décisions relativement aux barrières d'ordre tarifaire et non tarifaire au commerce.

Dans ce volume, le professeur Doern examine l'intervention gouvernementale dans l'industrie canadienne de l'énergie nucléaire. Il étudie en particulier les différences et les similitudes entre trois types d'intervention: propriété publique (pour la construction des réacteurs destinés à la production d'énergie); réglementation (relative à la santé professionnelle des mineurs d'uranium); contrats à long terme (pour la fourniture d'oxyde d'uranium à l'Hydro-Ontario). Tout en apportant une réponse à quelques-unes des questions relatives au caractère substitutif de certains instruments de politique publique, l'étude soulève d'autres questions à cet égard. Par exemple, si l'on y regarde de près, quelle distinction peut-on faire entre la propriété publique de telle ou telle industrie et, d'autre part, des contrats à long terme par lesquels le gouvernement achète virtuellement toute la production de cette industrie? Les différences ne sont-elles pas ici affaire de mots plutôt que de substance?

Dans les années à venir, la politique nucléaire acquerra vraisemblablement encore plus d'importance que ce n'est aujourd'hui le cas. L'ouvrage du professeur Doern, en nous aidant à comprendre le passé, nous prépare à mieux affronter l'avenir.

Michael J.L. Kirby, Président
Février 1980

Table of Contents

Preface	vii
Préface	viii
Acknowledgements	xiii
The Author	xiii
Executive Summary	xv
Abrégé	xix

INTRODUCTION   1

Chapter 1: GOVERNMENT INTERVENTION: CONCEPTS AND ISSUES   5

  (1) Intervention: Ideology, Objectives, and Paradigms   6
  (2) Nuclear Fuel Cycles and Physical and Technological Realities   8
  (3) Nuclear Policy Processes and Intervention   9
  (4) Instruments of Intervention   10
  Notes: Chapter 1   11

PART A: A PROFILE OF THE CANADIAN NUCLEAR INDUSTRY

Chapter 2: ECONOMIC CHARACTERISTICS   15

  (1) World and Domestic Nuclear Energy Supply and Demand   15
  (2) Domestic Nuclear Industry Characteristics   25
  Notes: Chapter 2   35

Chapter 3: POLITICAL CHARACTERISTICS   37

  (1) High Technology, CANDU, and the Use of Canadian Staple Resources for Economic Development   37
  (2) Public Opinion and Nuclear Interests   39
  (3) Foreign and Domestic Policy Relationships   42

(4) Public Sector-Private Sector Relations	45
(5) Federal-Provincial Relations	47
Notes: Chapter 3	49

Chapter 4: SCIENCE, TECHNOLOGY AND NUCLEAR POLICY 53

(1) Hypotheticality	54
(2) The Openness of the Regulatory Process	55
(3) Causal Knowledge and Political Perceptions	61
(4) Science and Technology Priorities: The Mix of Basic and Applied Research	62
(5) Deference to International Standard-Setting Bodies	62
(6) Science, Technology and Redistribution	63
Notes: Chapter 4	64

Chapter 5: ORGANIZATION, PROCESS AND POLICY 67

(1) Organization and Process: Towards Pluralization?	68
(2) Federal Statutory and Policy Arrangements	73
(a) Atomic Energy Control Act	74
(b) Atomic Energy Control Regulations	75
(c) Cabinet and Ministerial Policies	76
(i) Energy and Foreign Policy	76
(ii) Uranium Supply Policy	77
(iii) Safeguards Policy	77
(iv) Uranium Mining and Federal-Provincial Accommodation	78
(v) Licensing Policies and Procedures	80
(vi) Foreign Ownership or the Uranium Industry	81
(vii) Heavy Water	82
(viii) Waste Management	83
(ix) Other Federal Environmental Controls	84
Notes: Chapter 5	86

PART B: THREE CASE STUDIES IN GOVERNMENT INTERVENTION

Chapter 6: INTERVENTION AND INDUSTRIAL DEVELOPMENT: THE CANDU REACTOR PROGRAM   89

(1) Technical Issues in the 1950s   90
(2) Overseas Power Reactor Programs   93
   (a) United States   93
   (b) The United Kingdom   95
   (c) France   97
   (d) The Soviet Union   98
(3) The Canadian Nuclear Power Program   99
   (a) The Nuclear Power Demonstration Reactor   102
   (b) The Douglas Point Reactor   107
(4) The Douglas Point Decision: Technological Leapfrogging   110
(5) The Douglas Point Decision: A Reversal of Policy   112
(6) Intervention and Industrial Development   116
Notes: Chapter 6   120

Chapter 7: INTERVENTION, TECHNOLOGY AND REGULATION: THE URANIUM MINERS CASE   127

(1) The Economic Climate for Regulation   129
(2) The Regulatory Authorities   131
   (a) The Atomic Energy Control Board   131
   (b) The Ontario Regulatory Agencies   134
(3) The Determination of Exposure Standards and Compliance Practices   137
(4) Intervention, Technology and Regulation   143
Notes: Chapter 7   147

Chapter 8: INTERVENTION AND BARGAINING: THE ONTARIO HYDRO LONG TERM URANIUM CONTRACTS   151

(1) Main Events in the Contract Decision Process: 1972 to 1978   151
   (a) The Search for Secure Supply   151

(b) Supply Alternatives and the Possibility of Acquisition	152
(c) Federal Uranium Supply Policy and Bargaining Leverage	155
(d) Renegotiation and Broader Energy Trade-Offs	157
(e) The Select Committee Review: Obtaining Legitimacy	158
(f) Supply, Demand and Uncertainty	160
(2) Ontario Hydro and the Ontario Cabinet: Control, Independence and Intervention	164
(a) The Main Dimensions of Interdependence	164
(b) Intra-Cabinet Decision Routes	166
(3) The Denison and Preston Contracts	167
(a) Major Provisions	168
(b) Profit to the Producers	169
(c) The Advances	171
(d) Control, Security and Flexibility	172
(e) The Producers' Inducements to Bargain	175
(4) Intervention and Bargaining	177
Notes: Chapter 8	183

Chapter 9: CONCLUDING OBSERVATIONS   183

(1) The Three Case Studies: A Summary of Determinants	184
(2) General Observations about Intervention	190
(3) Intervention and the Future of the Canadian Nuclear Industry	193
Notes: Chapter 9	198

APPENDIX A	199
APPENDIX B	200
APPENDIX C	203

List of IRPP Publications

Acknowledgements

A study such as this is never the work of one person. I wish to thank my two research associates, Gordon Sims and Peter Akers, for their assistance in this study. Thanks are also due to my colleague Professor Bob Morrison as well as several graduate students in the School of Public Administration at Carleton University who took part in several nuclear policy seminars. Allan Tupper, David Brooks, Leon Katz and Bill Stanbury provided helpful comments on an earlier draft of this manuscript.

The financial support of the Institute for Research on Public Policy and the Institute of Public Administration of Canada (IPAC) is also gratefully acknowledged. The IPAC support will also contribute to a larger study of State Enterprise and Nuclear Policy to be published under their auspices.

The cooperation of numerous governmental officials and private individuals interested in the nuclear debate has also contributed to this work. Finally, I also wish to thank Martha Madsen at Carleton and Bill Stanbury of IRPP for their typing and editorial contributions respectively.

G. Bruce Doern
January, 1980

The Author

G. Bruce Doern is Director of the School of Public Administration of Carleton University in Ottawa. He is the author and editor of numerous articles and books on Canadian politics, public policy and administration, including Canadian Nuclear Policies (Institute for Research on Public Policy, 1980) with R.W. Morrison; The Regulatory Process in Canada (Macmillan of Canada, 1978); The Politics and Management of Canadian Economic Policy (Macmillan of Canada, 1978) with R.W. Phidd; and Science and Politics in Canada (McGill-Queen's University Press, 1972).

Executive Summary

This book examines several facets of government intervention in the Canadian nuclear industry by reviewing the general historical evolution of intervention since the Second World War and by a more detailed analysis of three case studies. The case studies are the public sector-private sector content of the initial CANDU reactor program in the 1950s, the regulation of the health and safety of uranium miners in the late 1960s and early 1970s, and the Ontario Hydro decision in 1978 to enter into longer-term (40 year) contracts for uranium for its power reactors.

The book does not examine all aspects of Canadian nuclear policy since its primary purpose is to analyze the nature of government intervention in the nuclear field. The three case studies each involve the use of a different <u>primary</u> instrument of public policy, namely public enterprise, regulation, and contractual arrangements. They provide and opportunity to probe more deeply into the possible substitutability of such instruments.

The book first outlines the central economic and political characteristics of the Canadian nuclear industry, examines the role of science and technology in the nuclear policy debate, and analyzes the organization and processes through which Canadian nuclear policy is made. The study draws particular attention to the degree to which the conscious <u>inaction</u> by government affects different interests favourably or adversely. It also stresses the need to examine intervention in a specific industry in an historical context and through a detailed analysis of the important decisions that have shaped the industry's development. Each of the case studies of nuclear decision-making is related to several major determinants of intervention. These include ideology, objectives, over-riding paradigms or ideas in existance in the nuclear policy field, physical and technological realities, economic factors, and intergovernmental and interagency relations. A number of generalizations about intervention emerge from, or are confirmed by, the study.

First, simple assertions that Canadian governments intervene largely on pragmatic grounds are unsatisfactory. While the three cases examined do <u>not</u> show that ideology <u>determines</u> intervention, they do show that it can foreclose the selection of certain instruments of intervention. Second, the study suggests the need for policy makers to look carefully at the choice and substitutability of the instruments of public policy. There may be very little to choose between the reactor program case where public ownership was used, aided by some contracting to the private sector, and the Ontario Hydro uranium contract case, where provincial ownership of uranium mines was foreclosed but long-term contracts were used in a way that the uranium companies became virtually the "chosen instrument" of government.

The third generalization that emerges adds further support to those who caution us about automatically equating the "public interest" with government intervention. The relationship between public and private interests is shown to be one that is far more complex with the public interest often being merely a convenient euphemism for the advancement of certain private interests. Finally, the case studies show that intervention cannot be divorced from perceptions of uncertainty and the willingness to bear risks. The study shows how, historically, the Ontario government and electricity users have been subsidized by Canadian taxpayers as a whole. The latter have borne most of the financial risks involved in nuclear power generation.

This book shows how a largely Canadian-owned high-technology industry has been fostered by a series of government decisions to intervene in the industry. It also raises concerns about how governments in Canada have, as a direct consequence, created a large vested interest in future nuclear expansion - a potentially unhealthy development at a time when the Canadian situation requires the widest possible search for alternative sources of energy.

The author supports the need for a vastly strengthened <u>Atomic Energy Control Act</u> along the lines suggested by the <u>Nuclear Control and Administration Act</u> (Bill C-14) which was tabled in 1977 and then allowed to die by the Trudeau Government in the face of provincial government criticism. He also expresses concern that the <u>Freedom of Information</u> Bill tabled by the Clark Government in the fall of 1979, paradoxically, may increase rather than decrease the already extreme secrecy surrounding nuclear policy and regulatory processes in Canada.

Abrégé

L'auteur examine dans cet ouvrage plusieurs aspects de l'intervention gouvernementale dans l'industrie canadienne de l'énergie nucléaire en retraçant l'évolution générale de cette intervention depuis la seconde guerre mondiale et en approfondissant trois études de cas. Ces études portent sur la participation respective des secteurs public et privé au programme du réacteur CANDU dans les années 50, sur la réglementation relative à la santé et à la sécurité des mineurs d'uranium à la fin des années 60 et au début des années 70 et sur la décision de l'Hydro-Ontario en 1978 de passer des contrats de fourniture d'uranium à plus long terme (quarante ans) pour alimenter ses réacteurs de puissance.

L'ouvrage n'épuise pas tous les aspects de la politique nucléaire canadienne: son objet principal est d'analyser la nature de l'intervention gouvernementale dans le domaine de l'énergie nucléaire. Chacune des trois études de cas reflète le recours particulier à un instrument primordial de politique publique: entreprise publique, réglementation et accords contractuels. Toutes trois offrent l'occasion d'examiner plus à fond l'interchangeabilité de ces instruments.

L'auteur esquisse d'abord à grands traits les caractéristiques économiques et politiques de l'industrie canadienne de l'énergie nucléaire, étudie le rôle de la science et de la technologie dans le débat sur la politique nucléaire, puis analyse l'organisation et les processus dont cette politique émerge. L'auteur s'attache particulièrement à définir la mesure dans laquelle l'inaction consciente des gouvernements favorise ou défavorise certains intérêts. Il souligne aussi la nécessité d'examiner l'intervention gouvernementale dans une industrie donnée à la lumière du passé et par une analyse détaillée des décisions importantes qui ont orienté le développement de l'industrie en cause. Chacune des trois études du processus décisionnel en matière d'énergie nucléaire se rapporte à plusieurs des facteurs déterminants de l'intervention gouvernementale, notamment les questions d'idéologie, les objectifs, les formules consacrées ou les idées reçues en matière de politique nucléaire, les réalités matérielles et technologiques, les facteurs économiques et les relations tant entre gouvernements qu'entre institutions gouvernementales. Un certain nombre de généralisations émergent de l'étude ou y trouvent leur confirmation.

Tout d'abord, il ne suffit pas d'affirmer tout simplement que l'intervention des gouvernements est dictée par des motifs d'ordre purement pratique. S'ils ne montrent pas que les positions idéologiques déterminent l'intervention, les trois cas étudiés établissent en revanche que certains des instruments d'intervention peuvent être écartés pour ces raisons. Deuxièmement, l'ouvrage laisse entendre que les artisans de la politique nucléaire devraient, de toute nécessité, examiner soigneusement le choix et le caractère interchangeable des instruments de politique publique. Il y a sans doute bien peu à choisir entre le cas du réacteur CANDU, où l'on a recouru à l'entreprise publique, et, d'autre part, le cas des contrats de l'Hydro-Ontario pour la fourniture d'uranium, où la province a renoncé à la propriété des mines pour jeter son dévolu sur des contrats d'approvisionnement à long terme: ces contrats ont été utilisés de telle sorte que les sociétés d'exploitation minière sont devenues, à toute fin utile, l'"instrument choisi" du gouvernement.

La troisième idée générale qui se dégage de l'ouvrage renforce la thèse de ceux qui nous mettent en garde contre l'assimilation spontanée de l'"intérêt public" à l'intervention gouvernementale. Le rapport entre l'intérêt public et l'intérêt personel est infiniment plus complexe que cette adéquation ne propose, l'intérêt public servant fréquemment d'euphémisme pour désigner la promotion de certains intérêts particuliers. Enfin, il ressort des études de cas qu'on ne saurait divorcer l'intervention gouvernementale d'un certain sentiment d'inquiétude et d'une disposition à courir certains risques. L'ouvrage montre que, traditionnellement, ce sont les contribuables canadiens dans l'ensemble qui ont subventionné le gouvernement de l'Ontario et les utilisateurs d'électricité: ce sont eux qui ont assumé la plus large part des riques financiers qu'entraîne la production d'énergie nucléaire.

Il se dégage de l'étude que la suite des décisions qui ont amené l'intervention gouvernementale ont favorisé le développement d'une industrie de technologie supérieure et de propriété largement canadienne. L'étude exprime aussi certaines préoccupations quant à la façon dont les gouvernements du pays, comme conséquence directe de leurs interventions, ont enchaîné leur intérêt à l'expansion future de l'énergie nucléaire: cette orientation n'est pas sans risque à une époque où la situation du Canada exige qu'on recherche, de la façon la plus poussée, des sources énergétiques de remplacement.

L'auteur appuie la nécessité de renforcer sensiblement la <u>Loi sur le contrôle de l'énergie atomique</u>, dans l'esprit du projet de loi C-14 sur l'administration et le contrôle de l'énergie nucléaire, déposé sur le bureau des Communes en 1977 et relégué à l'oubli par le gouvernement Trudeau à la suite des critiques du gouvernement provincial. Il s'inquiète aussi que le projet de loi sur la liberté d'accès à l'information, déposé par le gouvernement Clark à l'automne de 1979, puisse, paradoxalement, intensifier au lieu de diminuer l'extrême secret qui entoure la politique nucléaire et les processus de réglementation au Canada.

Introduction

The purpose of this book is to examine critically the role of government intervention in the Canadian nuclear industry. Since this study is one of a series on regulation and government intervention,* the nuclear industry as a whole will be treated as a major industry case study. Through an examination of one industry over a thirty-year period and through a more detailed study of three decision case studies, it is hoped that we can learn more about the causes, rationale and consequences of government intervention in Canada.

The words "government intervention" evoke a wide range of positive and negative responses among Canadian citizens and decision-makers. Canadians have historically not been adverse to using government intervention in many forms. In the apparent "anti-government" climate of the late 1970s it is all the more essential that one address the issue of government intervention in a careful historical context. All recent "sloganeering" to the contrary, government intervention is not a simple subject.

This study's primary task is to enquire into government intervention in the nuclear industry by examining the general historical evolution of intervention since the Second World War and by a more detailed analysis of three intervention decision processes as case studies, namely the public sector-private sector content of the initial CANDU reactor program in the 1950s, the regulation of the health and safety of ura-

---

* A complete list of IRPP publications can be found at the end of the volume.

nium miners in the late 1960s and early 1970s, and the 1978 Ontario Hydro decision to enter into long-term contracts for the supply of uranium. These cases were selected partly because they span the three decades when ideas about nuclear power changed. They were selected also because each centres on the ultimate use of different primary instruments of intervention, public enterprise, regulation, and contractual incentives, respectively.

It will quickly be evident from Part A (Chapters 2 to 5) of this book that there are numerous other instances in nuclear policy where intervention/non-intervention choices were made by decision-makers. The other decisions include such critical areas as international safeguards, heavy water production, reactor safety, and the uranium cartel, to name a few. Hence this study, even in the context of examining one industry, is a limited one since several important intervention decisions are not examined in detail. A deliberate choice had to be made between a light and superficial look at as many as fifteen key decisions and a somewhat more detailed examination of a few decisions. The latter option was adopted but we will refer to the other issues in a more general way.

The extent to which one can generalize about government intervention from the nuclear experience is also undoubtedly limited by some of the unique features of the nuclear industry. First, it is perhaps the classic Canadian example of a state-dominated industry since its most powerful organizations, Atomic Energy of Canada, Ltd., Eldorado Nuclear Ltd., Ontario Hydro, and Hydro Quebec are all owned by governments. Second, it is linked at an international level to perhaps the most strategically sensitive and critical issue facing the world community, namely the proliferation of nuclear weapons. Finally, as the events at Three Mile Island in the United States have graphically shown, nuclear power is the symbol of the growing public concern about the social management of complex technologies.

The study is organized into four major sections. The remaining part of the introductory section will examine briefly a number of concepts and issues involved in government intervention. Section II of the study presents a background profile of the Canadian nuclear industry with separate chapters on its economic (Chapter 2) and political characteristics, (Chapter 3) on the role of science and technology (Chapter 4) and on the organisation of nuclear policy processes (Chapter 5). The three case studies (Chapters 6, 7, and 8) on intervention referred to earlier will be examined in Section III. Finally, in Section IV, some concluding observations (Chapter 9) will be presented about the determinants and consequences of intervention in the Canadian nuclear industry.

Chapter 1

Government Intervention: Concepts and Issues

Perhaps the standard reply to the question of why Canadian governments intervene in anything is that they do so on pragmatic rather than on ideological grounds. This is an adequate response for anyone who does not want to think about a complex subject. Pragmatism simply becomes a word under which one avoids asking other more difficult questions. In the late 1970s the idea of even pragmatic intervention by government has not been warmly applauded. Under a constant barrage of anti-government and anti-bureaucracy pressure in the latter 1970s, the federal government in its 1976 paper, The Way Ahead, was moved to assert that, henceforth, it would seek to effect change through "non-interventionist" approaches.[1] By this it meant that it would rely less on spending, regulation and bureaucratic solutions and more on persuasion and consultation. While a plausible case can be made for this view of intervention, it is a fundamentally inadequate one because it fails to acknowledge the possibility that government intervention can occur through a failure to act or through so-called non-decision.[2] In short, an individual, group or sector of society can be as adversely affected by the designed inaction of governments as by the overt actions of government.

A logical implication of this dual concept of intervention is that some kinds of intervention are difficult to discover. It also suggests that government intervention in any single policy field or industry can only be intelligently examined by following and observing policy processes and outcomes over long periods of time.

(1) Intervention: Ideologies, Objectives and Paradigms

Nuclear policies, as are so many "fields" of public policy, are multi-valued. That is, they invoke concern about a range of ideologies, objectives and paradigms and the ranking of these change at different times among different participants.

At the level of major competing political and economic ideologies (e.g., conservatism, liberalism and socialism) nuclear policy involves a concern about the proper role of governments and of markets. What aspects should be left to the market? The nuclear reactor element of the industry has been largely under public sector ownership and control whereas the uranium mining element has been largely, though not exclusively, under private sector ownership but subject to government regulation. In October 1979 the federal government of Joe Clark announced its intention to sell Eldorado Nuclear Ltd. to private buyers. This sale did not arise out of nuclear policy issues per se, but rather to help signal the Clark government's commitment to "less government." Our case studies will show that ideological considerations have been important in other instances in explaining both overt intervention, failure to intervene, and the instruments of intervention.

Within the umbrella of competing general ideologies about the proper role of governments and markets, there are of course a number of more specific objectives which also provide the normative justification for intervention by government. These objectives at times have included Canadian technological leadership and prestige, employment (especially high technology employment), national security, aid to third world countries, regional disparities, and conservation of energy. It is important to stress that these objectives encompass purposes for public policy in the nuclear _and_ in closely related policy fields such as economic and foreign policy.

Public policy, and hence government intervention in any policy field, is also influenced by what some observers have called "paradigms," that is, a series of principles which "express the current assumptions from which specific policy-making can proceed, ... limit the appropriate choice of policy instruments, and ... summarize the world view of the policy-making community."[3] Examples of such "paradigms" are the "Keynesian" paradigm in macro economic policy, the "preventive" versus "curative" assumptions about medical care, and the need for "universality" versus "selectivity" in social welfare programs. Such paradigms can sometimes be distinguished from the broader general ideologies already noted above. Paradigms change slowly over time but can function somewhat independently of the broader ideological "isms" since they may apply to a smaller cluster of policy issues or even to a single policy field.

The recent articulation of so-called "hard" and "soft" energy paths can be seen in this light. Amory Lovins has advocated a "soft" energy scenario by which he means energy policies based on conservation, renewable resources, decentralized energy technologies and a better matching of resources to end uses.[4] He asserts that other current approaches to energy development (including nuclear) have relied on non-renewable resources and centralized technologies and hence should be considered to be "hard" energy paths.

Such paradigms of contending ideas are almost always excessively simple but they are an important factor in understanding intervention at different times. The development of new or competing paradigms can be at different times opportunities for thought and learning or obstacles to thought. It is for this reason that the current and future nature of intervention in Canadian nuclear policy cannot be described or evaluated with a few glib generalizations. "Hard" and "soft" energy paradigms are not the first to have influenced nuclear policy. During the Second World War and its immediate aftermath the operating paradigm was clearly a concern for strategic security. During the mid- and late-1950s the "atoms for peace" concept began to influence the climate of governmental intervention and the ends to which it was directed.[5]

It is thus essential to appreciate that pragmatism does not explain much about government intervention in the nuclear field especially if pragmatism implies a form of reactive "muddling through."[6]
This is not to suggest that broader ideologies and ideas have been the sole determinant. This study will show that ideologies about the role of the state and paradigms within the policy field have sometimes influenced intervention particularly by foreclosing or "screening out" certain options. It will show, however, that underlying the cloud of supposed pragmatism is a shifting coalition of public and private interests, each appealing to both self interest and to selected ideas.

(2) Nuclear Fuel Cycles and Physical and Technological Realities

An understanding of intervention must be rooted in a knowledge of the technical realities under which a given industry functions. In the nuclear industry this begins with an appreciation of nuclear fuel cycles. Fuel cycles exist for CANDU natural uranium reactors, for research reactors, and for proposed thorium fuelled reactors. The mere description of each cycle shows the numerous physical points at which intervention might occur and where technologies of various kinds can effect the form and consequences of intervention. Appendix A on the "once-through" CANDU fuel cycle shows that there are many points along the cycle from the mining, milling, fabricating and refining stages to the manufacture of heavy water, power generation and spend fuel disposal (or possible recycling) stages, where governments have intervened and technological and policy controversies have emerged. As Appendix A also demonstrates, further controversy emerges over pending decisions to begin the reprocessing of spent fuel.

At virtually all points along the cycle there are economic benefits at stake as well as the socio-economic costs inherent in the management of such problems as waste, environmental safety and health. Moreover, similar diagrams could be outlined for other potential future fuel cycles, including partially enriched uranium, thorium and breeder fuel cycles. The several fuel cycles will not be described further in this volume since there are standard references which do this more completely than would be possible here.[7]

(3) <u>Nuclear Policy Processes and Intervention</u>

Because of the characteristics of the nuclear fuel cycle, it must be stressed that there are a number of policy arenas and processes to be considered. There is no single nuclear policy process. Rather there exist legislative, foreign-domestic, federal-provincial, government-industry, media, interagency and public interest group <u>processes</u> where numerous multi-lateral or bilateral bargains are struck. Moreover, the policy processes are reflected in, and often constrained by several statutes as well as diverse expenditure and regulatory decisions. In short, ends and means or policy substance and process are closely intertwined and are often indistinguishable from one another.

In all of these processes public authorities may choose to intervene or not to intervene. Hence, as we have stressed, policy may flow either from overt decisions or from failures to act. There may be other points, moreover, where policy is formally expressed and articulated but its application and administration is frustrated either by design or by a failure to endow authorities and agencies with the necessary resources to see it implemented successfully.

Nuclear intervention is also affected by the <u>spatial</u> location and <u>class and group</u> consequences of policy. Thus different views and different rankings of values often emerge from the urban consumer of nuclear-generated power, the rural population where nuclear power plants are located, the residents and workers of the hinterland "company town" where uranium mines are situated, and the distant foreign developing country which buys a CANDU reactor.

Nuclear policies are also influenced by contending values about the policy <u>process</u> itself. The nuclear policy process is not merely a means to other ends; it is itself the object of genuine dispute. Nuclear policies are especially susceptible to conflict over process because they are the preeminent modern symbol of a broad public concern about the public management of new and large-scale technologies including their strategic international implications. They involve a need to consider how public decision processes should be designed to ensure public participation as well as the participation of experts.

(4) Instruments of Intervention

An understanding of intervention also requires an appreciation of the range and types of instruments through which government can intervene. The analysis in this book will draw particular attention to the substitutability of instruments. The conventional tool kit of governing instruments includes expenditure, regulation (including taxation) and persuasion or exhortation.[8] Public ownership is also an instrument which governments can use. These instruments can be broken into much finer gradations of choice. Expenditure can involve myriad conditional grants, subsidies, direct transfer payments, and contracts. Regulation can include the granting or withholding of tax benefits (tax expenditures), and can involve the application of rigid rules and standards or vague "guidelines." Regulation can involve a wide range of penalties and sanctions. Persuasion too can take many forms, including information programs, ministerial speeches, subtle arm twisting, the symbolic reorganization of departments or the creation of new ones and the use of consultative forums and advisory bodies.

Such instruments of governing and hence intervention cannot be viewed merely as means since there are different incentives, costs, benefits, degrees of permanence and uncertainties involved in their use. In a democratic system, moreover, the sequence in which such instruments are used is often valued in itself, in that politicians are judged both on the basis of how they exercise power and influence as well as on the nominal objectives they pursue.

It is also important to appreciate that both before and after particular instruments of intervention are used politicians and other government officials are influenced by patterns of supply and demand for intervention by various economic, political and bureaucratic interests in society. Intervention never starts <u>de novo</u>. It builds on previous arrangements and institutional practices, and how successful previously used instruments have been and/or are <u>perceived</u> to have been in solving a problem. Intervention occurs, moreover, through <u>organizations</u> and such organizations, though influenced by their legal mandate, have a life of their own with strong instincts for survival and expansion.

This analysis of government intervention in the nuclear industry attempts to shed some light on an admittedly complex process. It examines intervention in the form of both overt action <u>and</u> inaction. It identifies some of the winners and losers from past intervention and shows where intervention in the future will have to occur. The three case studies in Part B (Chapters 6, 7, and 8) reveal the ideologies, paradigms, ideas and interests which influenced intervention in the nuclear industry. They also show the numerous forms and instruments through which both kinds of intervention occur. These instruments include public ownership, the use of contracts, the promulgation of regulations, the failure to ensure regulatory compliance, the funding of research, the failure to act on research results, the reorganization of agencies, often, but not always, for largely symbolic purposes.

NOTES: Chapter 1

1. Government of Canada, <u>The Way Ahead: A Framework for Discussion</u> (Ottawa, 1976), p. 32.

2. For recent analyses of the role of the state in Canadian economic life, see Leo Panitch ed. <u>The Canadian State</u> (Toronto: University of Toronto Press, 1977); R.W. Phidd and G. Bruce Doern, <u>The</u>

Politics and Management of Canadian Economic Policy (Toronto: Macmillan of Canada, 1978); and Allan Tupper, The Nation's Business: Canadian Concepts of Public Enterprise (unpublished Ph.D. thesis, Queen's University, Kingston, 1977). See also Herschel Hardin, A Nation Unaware: The Canadian Economic Culture (Vancouver, J.J. Douglas, 1974).

3. See Ronald Manzer, "Public Policies in Canada: A Development Perspective." Paper presented to Canadian Political Science Association, Edmonton, June 1975. The classic reference is T.S. Kuhn, The Structure of Scientific Revolutions (Chicago: University of Chicago Press, 1962).

4. Amory B. Lovins, Soft Energy Paths: Toward a Durable Peace, (Cambridge, Mass.: Ballinger, 1977).

5. See W. Eggleston, Canada's Nuclear Story (Toronto: Clark Irwin, 1965) and Gordon Sims, The Evolution of AECL (unpublished M.A. thesis, Institute of Canadian Studies, Carleton University, 1979).

6. C.F. Lindblom, "The Science of 'Muddling Through'", in A. Etzioni ed. Readings on Modern Organizations (Englewood, Cliffs, N.J.: Prentice Hall, 1969) pp. 154-165.

7. For a clear readable description of nuclear fuel cycles see Walter C. Patterson, Nuclear Power (London, Penguin, 1976).

8. A more elaborate formulation can be found in G. Bruce Doern, "Rationalizing the Regulatory Decision-Making Process: The Prospects for Reform" (Ottawa: Economic Council of Canada, Regulation Reference Working Paper, 1979). For different views on the instruments of governing, see G. Bruce Doern (ed.) The Regulatory Process in Canada (Toronto: Macmillan of Canada, 1978) Chapter 1; Ken Woodside, "Tax Incentives vs. Subsidies: Political Consideration in Governmental Choice," Canadian Public Policy, Vol. 2 (Spring, 1979) pp. 248-156; Albert Breton, The Economic Theory of Re-

presentative Government (Chicago: Aldine, 1974); and Douglas G. Hartle, Public Policy Decision Making and Regulation (Montreal: Institute for Research on Public Policy, 1979).

PART A: A PROFILE OF THE CANADIAN NUCLEAR INDUSTRY

Chapter 2

Economic Characteristics

The Canadian nuclear industry functions within the broader context of a highly interdependent world and Canadian energy economy. It is an economy in which considerable uncertainty exists as to forecasts of medium and longer term energy supply and demand, the impact of conservation measures, the substitution of fuels, and the strategic international trade in energy. This chapter presents a summary profile of the economic characteristics of the Canadian nuclear industry in the context of this broader energy economy. It does not present an exhaustive analysis, but rather a brief profile to assist the reader in examining the issues of government intervention on which this study focusses. The economic parameters of the industry are presented in two sections, world nuclear energy supply and demand, and domestic nuclear industry characteristics.

(1) <u>World Nuclear Energy Supply and Demand</u>

World energy use (all sources) is closely linked with population growth and economic growth, particularly the latter. Figure 2.1 shows the changing shares in recent years, and as forecasted of energy use among the industrialized states, the rapidly emerging countries (e.g., Korea, Iran, Brazil) and slower economic growth countries. It projects a marked decline of the OECD countries' share from approximately 60 percent to just over one third. The implications of these projected energy shares are potentially enormous.

Figure 2.1
World Population, Gross Domestic Product and Energy Use

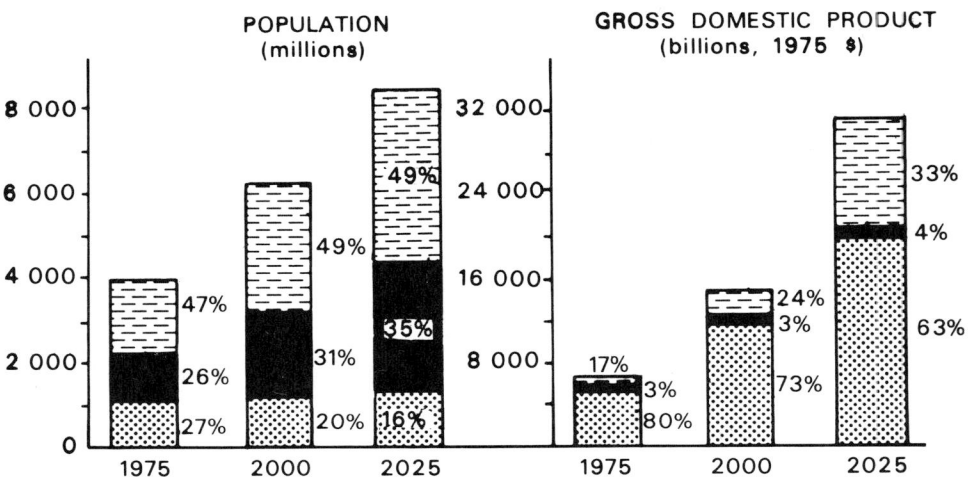

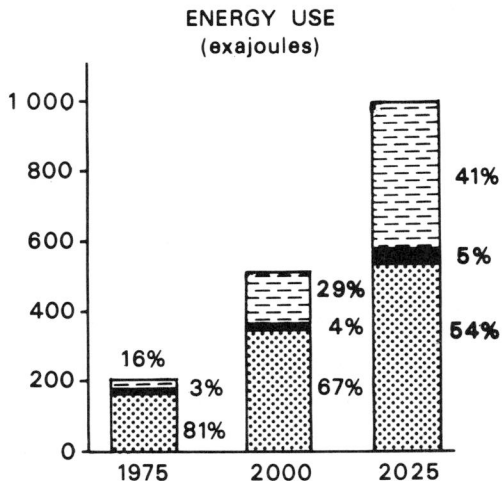

▨ WESTERN INDUSTRIAL, JAPAN, EAST EUROPE AND THE SOVIET UNION
■ SLOWER ECONOMIC GROWTH COUNTRIES
☰ RAPIDLY EMERGING COUNTRIES

Source: Energy Futures for Canadians (Ottawa: Department of Energy, Mines and Resources, 1978), p. 36.

Figure 2.2 illustrates the equally marked changes forecast in the share of the various resources which will make up the world supply of energy. It shows that the shares of oil and natural gas will decline significantly while there will be increases in the use of coal, nuclear and hydro power (but primarily nuclear) and other resources (renewable and byproduct forms of energy). The Department of Energy, Mines and Resources report from which the above forecasts are

Figure 2.2
Potential World Primary Energy Production

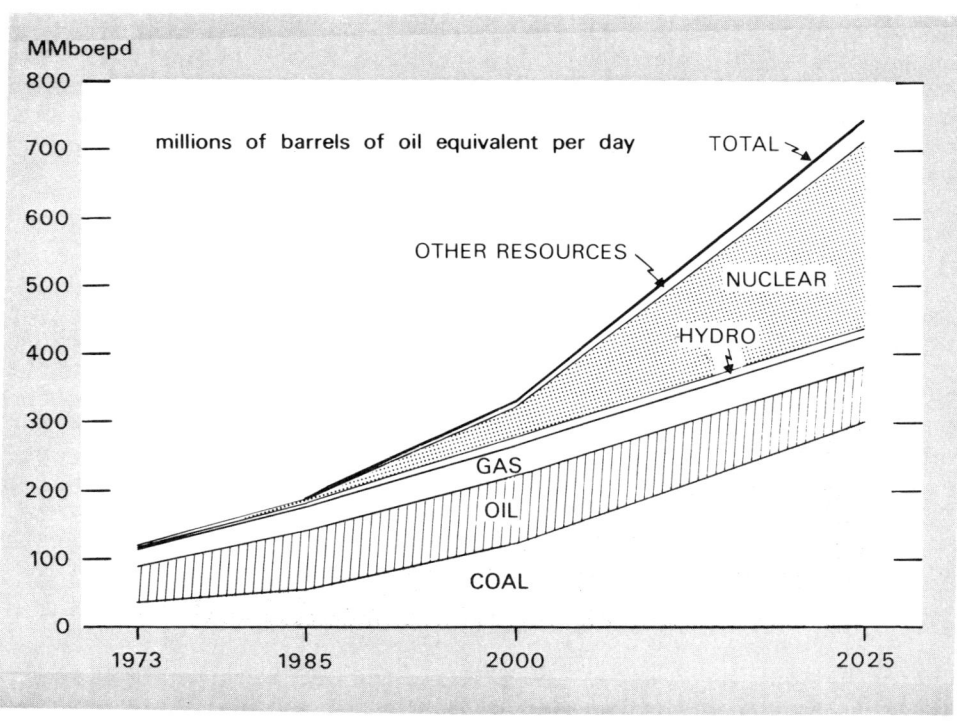

Source: see Figure 2.1 (p. 38).

drawn acknowledges the uncertainty created by public opposition to nuclear power but concludes that:

> Nuclear power is expected to make a very important contribution to future energy supplies. It is estimated that by 2025 up to 60 percent of all electricity might be generated by nuclear power. If this were to occur, nuclear energy and hydro power would supply virtually all of the base load electric power. Initially, nuclear energy will be used in the OECD countries, Eastern Europe and the USSR. By 1985, nuclear power could begin to make important contributions in developing countries such as Brazil, Mexico, India, Iran and South Korea. By 2025, half of the nuclear power might be generated outside the OECD countries. This points to problems related to the proliferation of nuclear materials and to waste management. Nuclear power (on an input basis) might grow from one MMboepd in 1973 to 11 by 1985, to more than 45 MMboepd by 2000, and to 280 MMboepd by 2025.[1]

While there is general agreement that nuclear energy will provide a much larger percentage of energy supply, there are vast differences in the degree of growth projected. An international workshop in 1976 on alternative energy strategies (WAES), in its published forecast of global energy prospects between 1985 and 2000 presented both "high economic growth" and "low economic growth" scenarios.[2] In recent years forecasts of new reactor capacity have been continuously revised downwards in all nuclear countries including Canada. Thus the large-scale demand for nuclear power envisaged after the 1973 OPEC oil embargo has not materialized.[3]

The Canadian CANDU Heavy Water reactor (HWR) supplies only about five percent of the current global nuclear reactor market. The other 95 percent is captured by Light Water Reactors (LWRs) either made in the United States or by other reactor vendors under license. The previously cited WAES study projected CANDUs share to be still a modest seven percent by the year 2000.[4] A recent assessment of the international nuclear reactor market summarized the situation as follows:

> Most of the industrialized countries either have, or wish to develop, their own nuclear manufacturing industry, so that reactor exports to those countries would most likely be under licence. The principle market for direct reactor sales lies in a small number of developing countries which are embarked on ambitious industrialization plans.... In buying their first reactors, countries may be choosing the reactor type on which their future programmes will be based. The market thus consists of a relatively small number of potentially large sales.
>
> The nuclear equipment suppliers - principally the United States, France, West Germany and Canada - all have considerable excess capacity in their domestic nuclear manufacturing industries. They need export contracts desperately. The market in reactors is a buyer's market. Fears have often been expressed that intense competition for sales might lead to a reduced concern for safeguard conditions.
>
> ... The CANDU is not indispensible. If it were unavailable its small share of the international market would be quickly occupied by the other suppliers although certain countries would be reluctant to lose access to the CANDU technology given its capability for autonomy.[5]

The uncertainties of energy and nuclear demand also effect the international uranium market, albeit in different ways. The supply of uranium is also influenced by the economics of exploration and development, mine and mill production, and enrichment (a

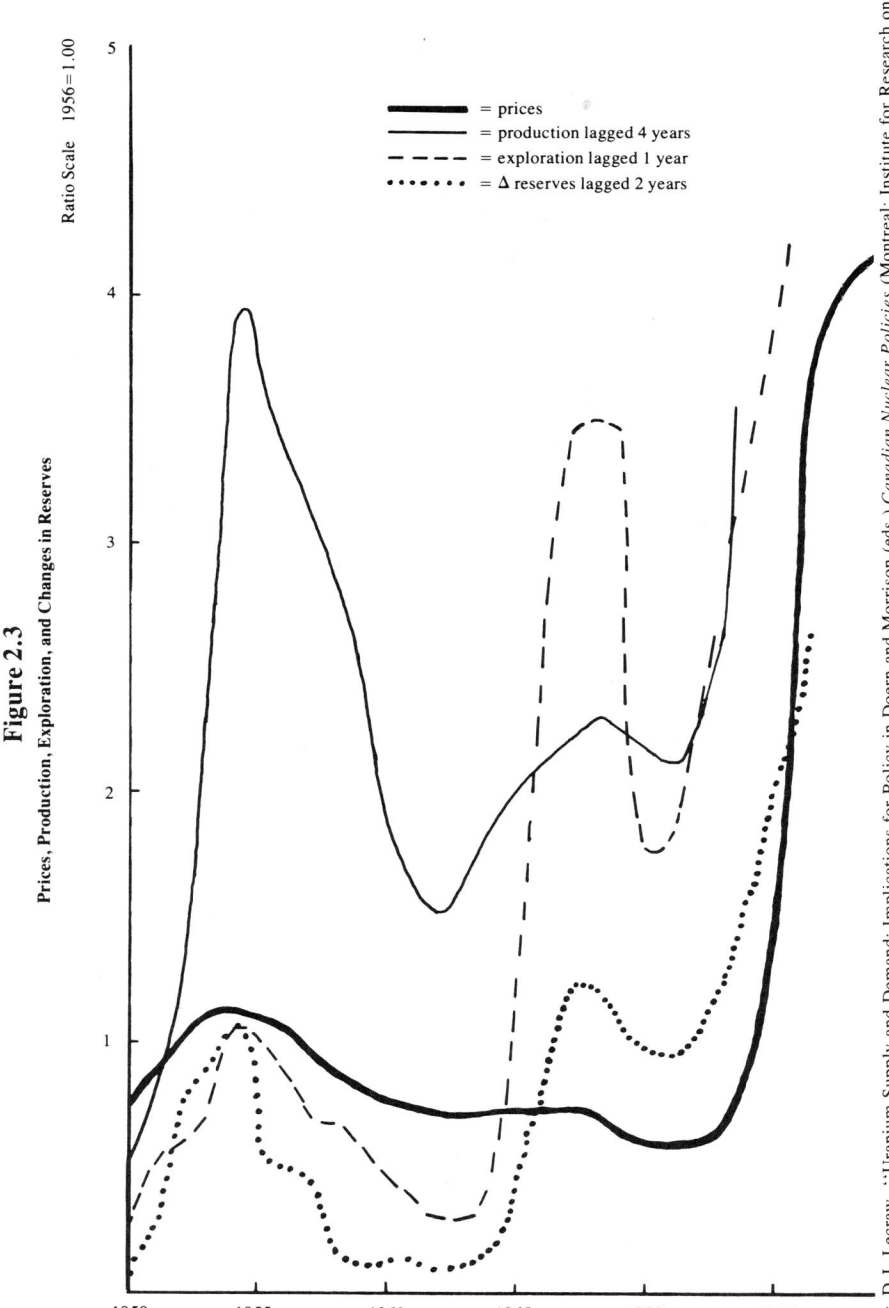

Figure 2.3
Prices, Production, Exploration, and Changes in Reserves

Source: D.J. Lecraw, "Uranium Supply and Demand: Implications for Policy in Doern and Morrison (eds.) *Canadian Nuclear Policies* (Montreal: Institute for Research on Public Policy, 1980) Ch. 5.

requirement for LWRs but not, at present, for CANDU HWRs). Supply is also influenced by a series of non-price variables.[6] In the short term (four years or less) price increases may result in producers, governments and customers responding by putting their uranium stockpiles on the market. Production itself is difficult to gear up in the short term. In a medium term period (five to ten years), some increased output can be achieved from existing mines and mills with only modest amounts of capital investment. In the long run (10-20 years), new mines which are economic at higher prices can be put into production, and new exploration can be begun. Because uranium producers have experienced earlier quite precipitous ups (1940s and 1950s) and downs (1960s) in the international uranium market, they are very conscious of the uncertainty of future price movements.[7] Figure 2.3 illustrates the lags and uncertainties of the uranium market.

Despite these problems, and in marked contrast to the international reactor market, the uranium market in the latter half of the 1970s has been much more of a seller's market. Few reactor vendor countries have uranium. The U.S. and France are viewed to be at best self-sufficient, but here as elsewhere, forecasts are not entirely reliable. Canada, Australia, and South Africa are currently the only countries with significant amounts of uranium for export. By the year 2000 it is expected that known uranium supplies will not cover expected demand.

The rapid increase in demand and prices, and hence in exploration has prompted most uranium producing countries to develop much more sophisticated programs to assess their reserves at various price levels. Figure 2.4 and 2.5 present some of these estimates. Figure 2.4 presents estimated "reasonably assured" and "estimated additional" resources, while Figure 2.5 shows <u>potential</u> production. Actual production up to 1978 has in fact been considerably lower.

The uranium market is also affected by the fact that the price of the uranium fuel is, relative to other energy sources, a small part of the cost of re-

Figure 2.4

Reasonably Assured Resources (1,000 tonnes U) / Estimated Additional Resources (1,000 tonnes U)
Data available 1 January 1977

Cost Range	$80/kg U ($30/lb U₃O₈) Reserves	$80-130/kg U ($30-50/lb U₃O₈)	80 US $/kg U ($30 $/lb U₃O₈)	80-130 US $/kg ($30-50 $/lb U₃O₈)
Algeria	28.	0	50	0
Argentina	17.8	24	0	0
Australia	289	7	44	5
Austria	1.8	0	0	0
Bolivia	0	0	0	0.5
Brazil	18.2	0	8.2	0
Canada[1]	167	15	392	264
Central African Empire[2]	8	0	8	0
Chile	0	0	5.1	0
Denmark (Greenland)	0	5.8	0	8.7
Finland	1.3	1.9	0	0
France	37	14.8	24.1	20.0
Gabon[2]	20	0.5	5	5
Germany, F.R.	1.5	0	3	0.5
India	29.8	0	23.7	0
Italy	1.2	0	1	0
Japan	7.7	0	0	0
Korea	0	3	0	0
Madagascar	0	0	0	2.0
Mexico[3]	4.7	0	2.4	0
Niger	160	0	53	0
Philippines	0.3	0	0	0
Portugal	6.8	1.5	0.9	0
Somalia[4]	0	6.2	0	3.4
South Africa	306	42	34	38
Spain	6.8	0	8.5	0
Sweden	1	300	3	0
Turkey	4.1	0	0	0
United Kingdom	0	0	0	7.4
United States	523	120	838	215
Yugoslavia	4.5	2.0	5.0	15.5
Zaire	1.8	0	1.7	0
Total (rounded)	1,650	540	1,510	590

[1] The material reported as Reserves is minable at prices up to $104/kg U and the other Reasonably Assured Resources are minable at prices between $104 and $156/kg U.
[2] Source of data: *Uranium: Resources, Production and Demand* (Paris: OECD, 1975).
[3] Data refer to resources "*in situ*," rather than recoverable.
[4] Costs of recovery are not known so the resources are arbitrarily assigned to the higher cost category.

Source: Uranium: Resources, Production and Demand, December 1977 (Paris: OECD, 1978).

Figure 2.5
Attainable Production Capabilities
(tonnes U)

	1977	1978	1979	1980	1981	1982	1983	1984	1985	1990
Argentina	130	280	360	360	310	310	390	600	600	600
Australia	400	500	500	500	1,800	4,600	8,300	10,600	11,800	20,000
Brazil	n.a.	n.a.	385	385	385	385	385	385	385	385
Canada	6,100	6,450	6,950	7,950	9,750	10,200	11,150	12,500	12,500	11,250
Central African Empire	0	0	0	0	0	1,000	1,000	1,000	1,000	1,000
France	2,200	2,850	2,850	2,850	3,350	3,600	3,600	3,600	3,700	4,000
Gabon	800*	(1,200)	1,200*	(1,200)	1,200*	1,200*	1,200*	1,200*	(1,200)	1,200*
Germany, F.R.	100	100	100	100	150	150	200	200	200	200
India	200*	200*	200*	200*	200*	200*	200*	200*	200*	200*
Italy	0	0	0	120	120	120	120	120	120	120
Japan	30	30	30	30	30	30	30	30	30	30
Mexico	0	20	90	170	550	550*	550*	550*	550*	550*
Niger	1,609	2,400	3,850	4,100	4,300	9,000	9,000	9,000	9,000	9,000
Philippines	0	0	38	38	76	76	76	38	0	0
Portugal	85	86	90	95	100	270	270	270	270	270
South Africa	6,700	8,800	9,700	11,700	11,700	12,900	12,800	12,600	12,500	12,000
Spain	191	191	339	678	678	678	678	678	1,272	1,272
Turkey	0	0	0	100	100	100	100	100	100	100
United States	14,700	19,300	20,300	22,600	26,300	31,200	32,300	34,300	36,000	47,000
Yugoslavia	0	0	0	0	120	120	120	180	180	440
Total (rounded)	33,000	42,000	47,000	53,000	61,000	77,000	82,000	88,000	92,000	110,000

( ) numbers taken from the 1975 Uranium Report.
* Estimated by the Steering Group of the Joint NEA/IAEA Working Party on Uranium Resources.
Source: *Uranium: Resources, Production and Demand*, December 1977 (Paris: OECD, 1978)

actor operation. Price is obviously not unimportant, but a strategically more important factor is security and reliability of supply. Morrison and Wonder offer this summary assessment of Canada's place in the uranium export market:

> ... the desire of the industrial countries for secure access to uranium resources gives Canada a certain amount of influence, since it has almost twenty percent of the world's known and estimated uranium resources. Much of this should become available for export, and Canada is considered a relatively stable supplier. Yet this influence is limited since attempts by Canada to impose onerous conditions on the export of its uranium could lead to retaliation in other areas by its uranium trading partners, and could also push them more rapidly toward uranium-conserving nuclear fuel cycles that might be more susceptible to diversion for weapons purposes.[8]

The medium and longer-term reactor and uranium markets will also be influenced greatly by technological change. Until 1977 one future technological scenario had always been quite clearly anticipated by world nuclear planners. The scenario envisaged was that irradiated fuel from enriched light water reactors (and from CANDUs) would be reprocessed and the uranium and plutonium recycled to achieve about a 30 percent gain in net uranium utilization. Development would meanwhile proceed on fast breeder reactors (FBRs) which, when complete, would allow the utilization of plutonium from earlier reactors in highly efficient fast breeder fuel cycles.[9] In 1977 President Carter declared a moratorium on such commercial reprocessing and launched the International Fuel Cycle Evaluation (INFCE) study. INFCE would specifically examine both advanced fuel cycle technologies and their proliferation characteristics with a view to minimizing the risk of weapons proliferation and ensuring security of long-term energy supply.

The basic motive behind the search for modified or new technologies and fuel cycles is the desire for secure sources of supply for energy generally and nuclear energy in particular. In the Canadian context the most feasible adaptation of CANDU technology is through the use of slight enrichment of the uranium in the CANDU fuel cycle and eventually adaptation to a thorium fuel cycle.

It is now increasingly clear that INFCE will not result in any major movement away from the Fast Breeder Reactor (FBR) scenario. Such developments will obviously effect Canada's reactor and uranium sales, albeit in ways which cannot yet be precisely determined. These are, moreover, not the only technological possibilities. New technologies for enrichment of uranium (heretofore largely lodged in the U.S.) are being developed and could result in new efficiencies in uranium use and in views about security of supply.

(2) Domestic Nuclear Industry Characteristics

The Canadian nuclear industry directly employs over 31,000 persons in numerous organizations involved in uranium mining and refining, research and development, engineering design, manufacturing, construction, utilities, and public administration.[10] Figure 2.6 shows a recent breakdown of employment in these sectors. About one third of the employment is of a highly technical nature and another third is in construction. Between 1965 and 1977 about $5.6 billion (in current dollars) had been invested in CANDU nuclear power.[11]

A recent study has estimated that the nuclear industry has a positive balance of payments of $335 million. This is primarily composed of the need not to import coal in Ontario as well as overseas reactor or reactor related orders ($50 million in 1977) and other nuclear service and equipment exports ($20 million in 1977). One estimate suggests that in 1988 the positive balance of payments contribution will have grown to $1.5 billion (1977 dollars) for fuel replacement alone.[12] Much, of course, depends on future domestic and foreign sales of reactors and uranium and

Figure 2.6

ESTIMATED DIRECT EMPLOYMENT IN THE CANADIAN NUCLEAR INDUSTRY, 1977

SECTOR	DIRECT EMPLOYMENT (PERSONS)	PERCENT
Uranium mining	500 [1]	1.6
Uranium refining	235 [3]	0.8
Research & development	3,280 [4]	10.5
Engineering & design	4,110 [4]	13.0
Manufacturing	6,000 [4]	19.1
Construction	11,450 [4]	36.4
Utilities[2] (operations, maintenance)	5,600 [4]	17.8
Public administration	250 [4]	0.8
TOTAL	31,425	100.0

Notes:

[1] Total employment in the uranium mining sector in 1977 is estimated at 5,000 persons. 10% of employment has been attributed to CANDU reactor fuel requirements.
[2] Total utility employment - Ontario Hydro, Hyro-Quebec, New Brunswick Power Corporation - exceeded 9,000 in 1977. 5,000 is the estimate of employment in operations and maintenance, training, etc.
[3] 50 percent of Eldorado Nuclear's reported Port Hope refinery employment.
[4] Leonard & Partners Limited estimates.

hence depends on the uncertain world and Canadian energy and economic forecasts already referred to earlier.

In 1978 Canada had 4,800 megawatts (MW) installed nuclear capacity (90 percent in Ontario).[13] Nuclear generated electricity grew from 0.1 percent of Canada's primary energy supply to 3.0 percent in 1977. As a percentage of electricity supply it has grown from

Figure 2.7

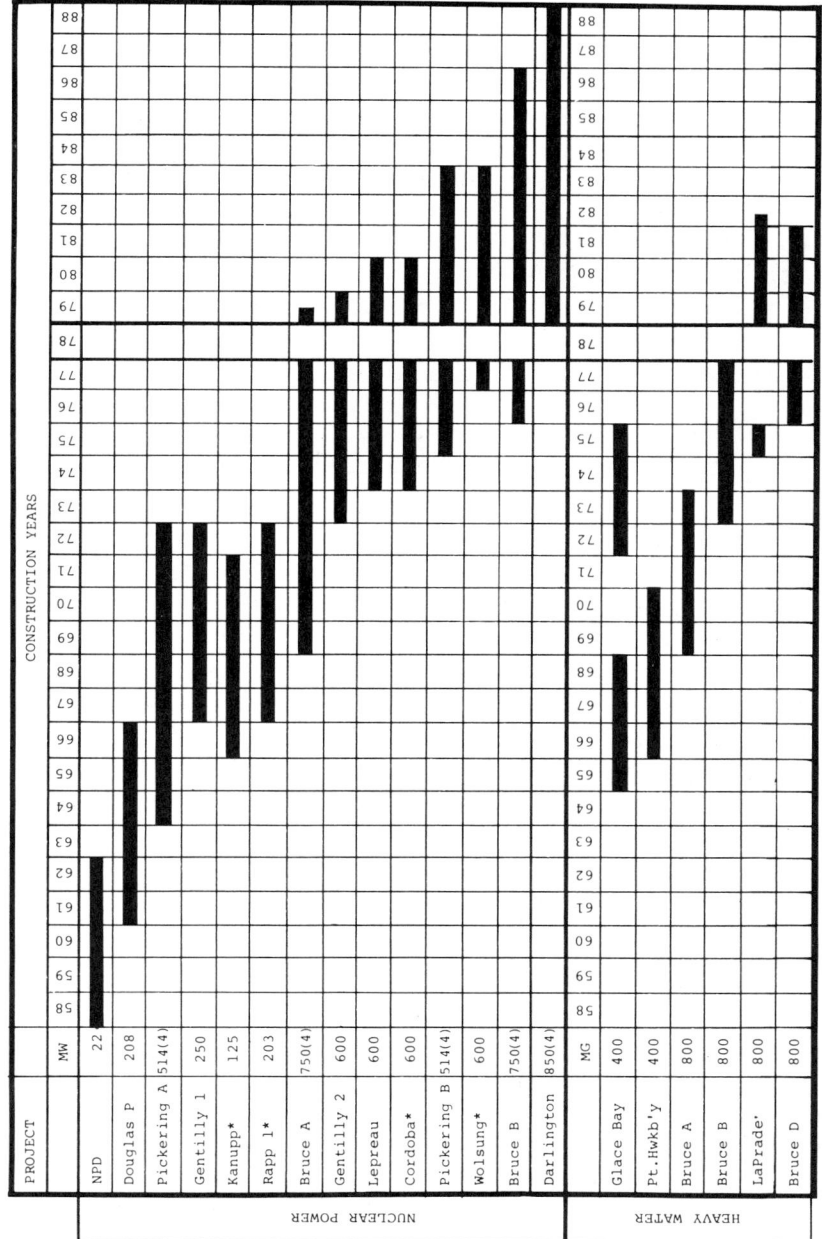

1.0 to 8.0 percent in the same time period. The Ontario figures are, of course, higher with nuclear contributing about 23 percent of electricity generation.

Figure 2.7 shows the confirmed nuclear power (including heavy water) program from 1958-1988. It includes both domestic and foreign reactor sales already constructed, under construction (in 1979) and firmly committed for construction. By 1988 it is expected that "on line" capacity will grow to 15,200 MW from the current 4,800 MW. These will be regionally distributed as follows:

YEAR	CANADA	ONTARIO	QUEBEC	NEW BRUNSWICK
1978	4,776	4,526	350	
1988	15,190	13,740	850	600

Since the publication of these figures, Ontario Hydro has revised its load forecasts downward and therefore some doubt exists as to the building of some of the Darlington units.[14]

Figure 2.8 provides a more detailed list of Canada's domestic reactors showing the high degree to which Ontario Hydro and AECL, in contrast to the American industry, assumed direct responsibility for the architectural, engineering and construction phases of the reactor program. These should be seen in relation to the broader structure of the industry summarized in Figure 2.9. It should be stressed, however, that the manufacturing and construction share of the total commissioned cost of a CANDU nuclear power station is between 50% and 57% and that much of this is provided by the private sector.[15] This public/private share in the operation of the industry must be taken into account when interpreting Figure 2.10. It shows a rough estimate of Canada's investment in nuclear power between 1965 and 1977. The investment totals $5.6 billion in current dollars, or $8.4 billion 1977 dollars. It does not cover earlier subsidized costs before 1965.

Figure 2.8

CANADIAN DOMESTIC REACTOR PROGRAM

PLANT	NET MWe	TYPE	REACTOR SUPPLIER	GENERATOR SUPPLIER	ARCHITECT ENGINEER	CONSTRUCTOR	CONSTRUC- TION STAGE (%)	COMMERCIAL OPERATION orig. schedule	actual or expected
New Brunswick Electric Power Commission									
Point Lepreau (Bay of Fundy, N.B.)	630	PHWR	AECL	H-P	AECL/CTL/ Utility	Utility	60	10/79	12/80
Ontario Hydro									
Douglas Point (Tiverton Ont.)	206	PHWR	AECL	AEI	OH/AECL	OH	100	7/65	9/68
Pickering 1 (Pickering Ont.)	515	PHWR	AECL	H-P	OH/AECL	OH	100	11/70	7/71
Pickering 2 (Pickering Ont.)	515	PHWR	AECL	H-P	OH/AECL	OH	100	10/71	12/71
Pickering 3 (Pickering Ont.)	515	PHWR	AECL	H-P	OH/AECL	OH	100	10/72	8/72
Pickering 4 (Pickering Ont.)	515	PHWR	AECL	H-P	OH/AECL	OH	100	10/73	5/73
Bruce 1 (Tiverton Ont.)	740	PHWR	AECL	H-P	OH/AECL	OH	100	6/77	9/77
Bruce 2 (Tiverton Ont.)	740	PHWR	AECL	H-P	OH/AECL	OH	100	9/75	9/77
Bruce 3 (Tiverton Ont.)	740	PHWR	AECL	H-P	OH/AECL	OH	100	6/78	2/78
Bruce 4 (Tiverton Ont.)	740	PHWR	AECL	H-P	OH/AECL	OH	100	6/79	1/79
Pickering 5 (Pickering Ont.)	516	PHWR	AECL	H-P	OH/AECL	OH	70	4/80	5/82
Pickering 6 (Pickering Ont.)	516	PHWR	AECL	H-P	OH/AECL	OH	65	1/81	12/82
Pickering 7 (Pickering Ont.)	516	PHWR	AECL	H-P	OH/AECL	OH	60	10/81	5/83
Pickering 8 (Pickering Ont.)	516	PHWR	AECL	H-P	OH/AECL	OH	55	7/82	10/83
Bruce 5 (Tiverton Ont.)	756	PHWR	AECL	CGE	OH/AECL	OH	30	10/82	10/83
Bruce 6 (Tiverton Ont.)	756	PHWR	AECL	CGE	OH/AECL	OH	30	7/83	7/84
Bruce 7 (Tiverton Ont.)	756	PHWR	AECL	CGE	OH/AECL	OH	20	4/84	4/84
Bruce 8 (Tiverton Ont.)	756	PHWR	AECL	CGE	OH/AECL	OH	20	1/85	1/87
Darlington 1 (Newcastle Twp.Ont.)	881	PHWR	AECL	BBC	OH/AECL	OH	0	8/86	2/86
Darlington 2 (Newcastle Twp.Ont.)	881	PHWR	AECL	BBC	OH/AECL	OH	0	11/85	5/87
Darlington 3 (Newcastle Twp.Ont.)	881	PHWR	AECL	BBC	OH/AECL	OH	0	5/87	11/89
Darlington 4 (Newcastle Twp.Ont.)	881	PHWR	AECL	BBC	OH/AECL	OH	0	2/88	8/90
Hyro Quebec									
Gentilly 1 (Becancour Que.)	250	BLWR	AECL	BBC	AECL/SNC/ MECO	HQ	100	/71	5/72
Gentilly 2 (Becancour Que.)	638	PHWR	AECL	GE	AECL/CTL/HQ	HQ	78	/79	3/81

Source: tabulation by author.

Figure 2.9
BROAD STRUCTURE OF CANADIAN NUCLEAR INDUSTRY

SECTOR		MAJOR ORGANIZATIONS INVOLVED
1) MINING & REFINING		1) MINING COMPANIES REFINING COMPANY (ELDORADO NUCLEAR)
2) RESEARCH & DEVELOPMENT		2) AECL UTILITIES UNIVERSITIES PRIVATE SECTOR
3) ENGINEERING & DESIGN	NUCLEAR POWER STATIONS + HWP	3) AECL UTILITIES PRIVATE SECTOR
4) MANUFACTURING - equipment - structural materials - other		4) PRIVATE MANUFACTURING COMPANIES
5) CONSTRUCTION		5) UTILITIES PRIVATE SECTOR CONTRACTORS AECL
6) OPERATIONS & MAINTENANCE		6) UTILITIES
7) PUBLIC ADMINISTRATION		7) AECB FEDERAL GOVERNMENT PROVINCIAL GOVERNMENTS UNIVERSITIES

Source: Leonard and Partners, *Economic Impact of Nuclear Energy Industry in Canada*, (Ottawa, 1978) p. vi-1.

Figure 2.10

Estimated Investment in CANDU Nuclear Power Program
(1965 - 1977 ($ million)

	ESTIMATED EXPENDITURE		
COMPONENT	DOMESTIC	FOREIGN	TOTAL
Current dollars			
Construction - NPS	2,966	368	3,334
Construction - HWP	1,174	150	1,324
Construction - NPS & HWP	4,140	518	4,658
Research & Development	946	--	946
TOTAL	5,086	518	5,604
1977 dollars			
Construction - NPS	4,467	554	5,021
Construction - HWP	1,683	215	1,898
Construction - NPS & HWP	6,150	769	6,919
Reseach & Development	1,490	--	1,490
TOTAL	7,640	769	8,409

Note: Because of a lack of data, only the period 1965 to 1977 was covered. No account was taken, therefore, of expenditures and investment by private-sector companies and crown corporations to service the nuclear power program prior to 1965.

Source: Leonard and Partners Limited, Economic Impact of Nuclear Energy Industry in Canada (Ottawa, 1978) V-14.

The prospects for future foreign sales are somewhat cloudy although it is agreed that foreign sales are needed if the industry is to be kept on an even keel, particularly in terms of surviving the lull in sales/construction in 1980.[16] Negotiations for possible CANDU sales are continuing with a number of countries including Romania, Argentina, South Korea, Italy, Japan, and Mexico. Previous foreign sales summarized in Figure 2.11.

The Heavy Water component of the nuclear industry has suffered from a period of severe shortage of supply (due to technical difficulties), but now faces a serious over supply situation. In 1988 there will be six heavy water plants in operation. It is questionable whether the La Prade Quebec plant will be built. It is currently a subject of federal-provincial conflict following the federal government's decision in August 1978 to put it into "mothballs." The mid-1980 total of 4,000 tonnes capacity is considered sufficient to meet demand into the 1990s.[17]

The Ontario Royal Commission on Electric Power Planning (the Porter Commission) conducted a comparative life cycle cost comparison of nuclear versus coal generated electrical power. Its calculations went further than most in including all the fuel cycle costs from exploration and mining through to station decommissioning and waste disposal. It concluded that

- CANDU units in 850 MW capacity range are the obvious economic choice of Ontario Hydro's base load generation (but suggested a delay in using larger units until at least the end of the century)

- Once constructed, nuclear power with its high capital costs and low operating costs is less susceptible than coal to inflation and relatively insensitive to fuel costs. The fuel cost ratio of nuclear power to coal power per kWh generated is roughly 1:9.[18]

It went on to caution, however, against major nuclear expansion, not only because of social concerns, but

Figure 2.11

Overseas Sales of CANDU Power Reactors in 1965-1978
($ million current)

COUNTRY	SIZE (MW)	Designation	Construction Period	APPROXIMATE VALUE	
				Total Industry Effort[1]	Total Canadian Effort[2]
Pakistan	125	Kanupp 1	1966-72	122	80
India	208	Rapp 1	1967-73		
Argentina	600	Cordoba 1	1974-81	313	235
South Korea	600	Wolsung 1	1977-82	313	235
TOTAL OF ABOVE	1,533			$748	$550

Notes:

[1] Total industrial effort is estimated value of contracts for buildings, equipment, engineering/design, construction, installation, heavy water and fuel.
[2] Canadian industrial effort is estimated value of Canadian content of total industrial effort contracts.

Source: AECL estimates.

---

also on economic grounds because of a concern for excessive load growth forecast by Ontario Hydro and the difficulties of obtaining sufficient capital.

Some have seriously questioned the direct "nuclear versus coal economics" comparison arguing that the choice is not nuclear or coal but some broader more judicious mix of several energy sources including renewable ones.[19] While the nuclear versus coal "numbers" are not themselves in serious dispute, the value of the assumptions behind the choice of what to compare are in dispute.

The uranium component of the Canadian nuclear and energy economy has been without doubt the most bullish in recent years. Canada has been a prime beneficiary of a massive world-wide search for secure uranium supplies. Foreign governments, their energy utilities, and private concerns (including the giant multi-national oil companies) have invested heavily in uranium exploration in Canada. As noted earlier, Canada produces about 20 percent of the world's uranium. There are six uranium companies actively producing in Canada, Rio Algom Limited, Denison Mines Limited, Madawaska Mines Limited, Eldorado Nuclear Limited, and Gulf Minerals Canada Limited. It is expected that this number will increase to about ten. Despite recent expansion it is not expected that the 1959 industry record output of 12,300 tonnes will be achieved until 1984. Production in 1977 was 5,800 tonnes. Over 90 percent of Canadian production has been exported, with exports growing from $34 million in 1970 to $237 million in 1977.[20] The uranium mining industry employs about 5,000 persons. About 10 percent of the total accounted for by CANDU fuel requirements. The federally owned Eldorado Nuclear Limited employs about 478 persons in uranium refining.

Recent uranium (U_3O_8) prices of $40 per pound are a far cry from the severe market slump of the 1960s and early 1970s. The expansion of the 1950s had been geared mainly for the U.S. weapons stockpile program. When this market was largely closed off by American policy, Canadian governments supported the domestic program first through special stockpiling arrangements and, when other marketing efforts failed, with the sponsorship of an international uranium cartel. By the time the cartel was in operation, market prices were already moving upward at an accelerating rate, again partly due to U.S. policy. Within a very brief period of time uranium prices soared from as little as $4 per pound of U O to over $40.[21]

As was the case in the discussion of world uranium supply and demand there are numerous uncertainties in the Canadian market. Expectations of future prices vary greatly.

In general then the Canadian nuclear industry, however much it may be a technically respected and successful industry, has not been "commercially" successful in the pure market sense of that word. This is especially the case in the reactor component of the industry which has been heavily subsidized by government.

NOTES: Chapter 2

1. James E. Gander and Fred W. Belaire, Energy Futures for Canadians (Ottawa: Department of Energy, Mines and Resources, 1978) p. 40.

2. Energy: Global Prospects 1985-2000, Report of the Workshop on Alternative Energy Strategies (New York: McGraw-Hill, 1976).

3. See U.S. House of Representatives, Committee on Government Operations, Nuclear Power Costs (Washington, D.C.: USGPO, April 1978) and Charles Komanoff, Rising Costs of Nuclear Power Plants (New York: Komanoff Energy Associates, September 1978).

4. Energy: Global Prospects 1985-2000, op. cit., p. 196.

5. R. Morrison and E. Wonder, "Canada's Nuclear Export Policy" in G. Bruce Doern and R. Morrison (eds.) Canadian Nuclear Policies (Montreal: Institute for Research on Public Policy, 1980), Chapter 4.

6. Donald J. Lecraw, "Uranium Supply and Demand: Implications for Policy" in Doern and Morrison, op. cit., Chapter 5.

7. Department of Energy, Mines and Resources, A Brief Submitted to the Cluff Lake Board of Inquiry. Regina, Saskatchewan, April 1977.

8. Morrison and Wonder, op. cit., p. 6.

9. Walter C. Patterson, Nuclear Power (London: Penguin Books, 1976).

10. Leonard and Partners Ltd., Economic Impact of Nuclear Energy Industry in Canada. Executive Summary (Ottawa: Leonard and Partners Ltd., 1978) p. 14.

11. Ibid., p. 7.

12. Ibid., p. 16.

13. Ibid., p. 2.

14. Royal Commission on Electric Power Planning, A Race Against Time (Toronto: Ontario Queen's Printer, 1978) Chapters 2 and 3.

15. Leonard and Partners, Ltd. Economic Impact of Nuclear Energy Industry in Canada. Detailed Report. (Ottawa, 1978) pp. 21-25, 2nd 21-31.

16. See A Report By the Task Force on CANDU Export Marketing. (Ottawa, 1978).

17. Leonard and Partners Ltd., Executive Summary, op. cit., p. 7.

18. Royal Commission on Electric Power Planning, A Race Against Time (Toronto: Ontario Queen's Printer, 1978) p. xiii and pp. 103-124.

19. David B. Brooks, "Commentary on the Political Economy of Nuclear Policy" in Doern and Morrison, op. cit., Chapter 4.

20. Leonard and Partners, op. cit., p. 8.

21. Department of Energy, Mines and Resources, op. cit., p. 18.

Chapter 3

Political Characteristics

The economic profile presented in Chapter 2 provides an initial indication of the political issues that must be resolved and balanced. They do not, however, provide a full appreciation of the politics of Canadian nuclear policy and intervention. For this we require an understanding of a number of other issues and processes including: the relations between CANDU high technology, staple resources and Canadian economic development; public opinion and nuclear interest groups; foreign and domestic policy relationships; public sector-private sector relations; federal-provincial relations; and inter-agency relations (an issue introduced here but the subject of a more detailed analysis in Chapter 5).

(1) High Technology, CANDU, and the Use of Canadian Staple Resources for Economic Development

The nuclear industry represents the best example of a Canadian high technology industry, a type of industry essential for future economic growth. It is also based, however, on a staple resource, in this case uranium. In the past, Canada has frequently built much of its economic prosperity on other staples.[1]

The "high technology" and "staple" routes to economic development are perhaps uniquely combined in the nuclear industry. This is important because current nuclear policy is being developed at a time of Canadian economic vulnerability. This vulnerability is characterized by the relative absence, in comparison with other western countries, of high-technology-based industries, the sharp decline of the employment-intensive secondary manufacturing sector, the high dependence on foreign trade including, in particular, trade in primary renewable and non-renewable resources, to overcome unfavourable trade balances in other sectors, and a general economic malaise characterized by high unemployment and rates of inflation and a breakdown in the earlier Keynesian consensus on how to "manage" the economy.[2]

It can be argued that Canadian-developed CANDU nuclear technology is Canada's last and/or best chance for developing and maintaining a high-technology-based and internationally competitive and respected industry. Such an argument is rarely explicitly articulated, but there can be little doubt that senior decision makers consciously and subconsciously view our nuclear technology and the nuclear technological community as an asset not to be squandered. Ever since the cancellation of the Avro Arrow in the late 1950s and the subsequent damaging effect it had on the advanced-technologically-based aeronautics industry, government decision-makers have been aware of the need to avoid further similar technological debacles.[3] Their awareness has been enhanced by the consistent failure over the last decade, the advocacy of science policy enthusiasts and ministries to the contrary notwithstanding, to find major technological "lead" sectors. Although useful developments have occurred in such fields as space and oceans technology it remains the case that nuclear technology often seems to be perilously alone. We are very close to a technological strategy of "putting all the eggs in one basket." Concentration and selection are important features of policy strategy for a middle industrial power like Canada but they also are replete with risks.[4]

None of the above is intended to suggest that the nuclear industry is a major "lead" sector in a direct economic sense since as we have seen in Chapter 2 it is not, comparatively speaking, a major employer among Canadian industries. Its importance as a <u>symbolic</u> lead sector in high technology industry cannot, however, be doubted. In the current economic climate, moreover, a marginal-employment industry is even more important especially when the industry contains such a high proportion of highly qualified manpower in its total employment population. The psychological importance of this argument is especially reinforced in the late 1970s by the concurrent re-emergence of the economic value of staple resources, especially uranium, in the face of declining industrial (manufacturing) employment.

(2) Public Opinion and Nuclear Interests

During the 1950s and 1960s public opinion in Canada about nuclear policy could be said to consist of a high degree of deference, awe and mystery. While there has always been a strong concern about nuclear weapons, the domestic power and research program operated largely in an environment of benevolent deference to scientific authority and expertise.[5] There was some criticism of the CANDU project by the technical trade press, but this was largely over Canada's decision to go it alone with CANDU. There were pro-nuclear interests but these were centered in AECL and Ontario Hydro and they tended to be interests expressed in the private counsels of government.[6] This situation changed drastically in the 1970s and followed a pattern of development roughly equivalent to that in order western states with developed nuclear industries.[7] A number of nuclear critics and public interest groups began to emerge. These included Energy Probe, and the Coalition for Nuclear Responsibility, organizations with fragile financial support but with many competent and dedicated persons concerned about nuclear and related energy and environmental issues.[8] Pro-nuclear interest groups such as the Canadian Nuclear Association (CNA) also began to strengthen their resolve to defend their interests against what they felt was unwarranted criticism by anti-nuclear groups and by the press. Increased media coverage showed much public ignorance and later, in 1977, reflected a slight majority opinion among Canadians against nuclear power.[9] The Three Mile Island accident in the U.S. early in 1979 contributed to these trands in public opinion. Unpublished polls conducted by AECL showed that opposition increased only marginally after Three Mile Island but increased markedly after media exposure to the Ontario Select Committee on Hydro hearings on reactor safety later in the summer of 1979.[10]

For most of the 1970s the pro and anti-nuclear interests were relative political novices, at least as far as their public political tactics can be judged. The nature of their debate served to sharpen and stake out different value positions about technology generally, and nuclear technology in particular. It also served to cloud, or indeed ignore, other issues. The first phase of political exchange beginning in the mid-1970s was characterized by presentations of a very stereotyped view of the other side. The anti-nuclear groups tended to view the Canadian nuclear technological community as uncaring, over-confident, technological elitists, while the pro-nuclear interests saw their opponents as ill-informed amateurs who preferred to appeal to emotions rather than deal with facts. Though both interests were aware of the more complex tactics employed in other countries they adopted a quite simple set of arguments and tactics which were perhaps inevitable given the closed nature of Canadian nuclear policy processes.

The position of the nuclear technological community was typified in the response of the CNA. The CNA countered its nuclear critics by arguing that anti-nuclear interests were being emotional and irrational. It commissioned and published large public opinion and elite opinion surveys on the tactical assumption that the more facts and knowledge people had about nuclear power the more favourable would be their view of it.[11] In taking this approach it demonstrated its belief in the existence of a strong causal link between "knowledge" and political support. While one would always like to think that some such link exists, these early strategies displayed a sense of innocence about the complexity of real political processes and hence paralleled earlier excursions into the public political arena by the technological and scientific community in the 1960s.[12] In short, the pro-nuclear interests were very unscientific about developing an understanding of the relationships between knowledge and political support. Strong traces of this residue of political simplicity exist today. Moreover, despite its proclaimed faith in the value of public education in generating current and future support for its industry, the pro- nuclear interests (like many other interests) are very selective in their faith in the public. Their positions on opening the nuclear tions on opening the nuclear policy process to wider public have been at best ambivalent, and at worst, in outright opposition.

For their part, the anti-nuclear groups tended too often to want to "out-science" the nuclear community. This strategy had some value but was almost certainly doomed to have a limited impact, given the virtual domestic monopoly of expertise possessed by the Canadian nuclear community. While anti-nuclear groups have properly criticized the closed nature of Canadian nuclear decision and regulatory processes,[13] they have often been inexplicably reluctant to learn much from the experience of their counterparts in other countries. These groups have directed their criticisms away from the narrower (though not unimportant) scientific and technical questions, where pro-nuclear technologists have the clear advantage, and into other potentially more vulnerable economic aspects of the nuclear industry (including its heavily subsidized nature) and into the important security questions related to terrorism. The future threat or use of nuclear terrorism in _any_ part of the world would quickly arouse public opinion in all parts of the western world.

Both pro and anti-nuclear interests have entered lately into a second phase in their political tactics and arguments. Both seem willing to extend and broaden their debate into a wider realm of economic and political reality, but without conceding the underlying contending values about the social consequences of nuclear technology which both staked out in the first phase of their political exchange.[14] The future politics of Canadian nuclear policy will have to build on this recent process of maturity in which nuclear policy analysis is perceived less exclusively as a problem of science and government and is more critically linked to Canadian economic policy generally, and to the broad energy and resource strategies of federal and provincial governments.

(3) Foreign and Domestic Policy Relationships

Needless to say, there are many potential conflicts to mediate and bargains to be struck between the foreign and domestic aspects of Canadian nuclear policy. These conflicts also help to determine the degree and the nature of government intervention.[15] Our earlier analysis has already shown that there are strong economic interests pressing for exports and for direct and indirect government aid in concluding such export arrangements. This interest is strong both in reactor sales and in uranium exports. Political pressure for sales also exists and is indeed often indistinguishable from economic pressures. These pressures arise from other countries who may view Canadian uranium supplies as a strategic necessity or who may be interested in CANDU to get access to advanced technology. Concern in the late 1970s over secure energy supplies make these pressures all the more prevalent since nuclear related sales will also increasingly be tied to other energy and related "swaps" or product trade-offs.[16]

Pressure against export sales has been considerable, particularly since India's explosion of a nuclear device in 1974 constructed in part out of a research reactor bought from Canada. The Indian explosion ended an era of relative Canadian innocence and shattered faith in the earlier somewhat simplistic belief about "atoms for peace." Concern about the proliferation of nuclear weapons to other states in areas of regional and/or global strategic tension was heightened. Canada responded by demanding tougher full scope safeguards and backed-up its claims by unilaterally placing an embargo on uranium sales to western Europe and Japan during 1977. Such unilateral action, though admirable in many respects, was viewed by Canada's nuclear customers as unwarranted and unnecessary.

Foreign and domestic policy factors are now maintained in a somewhat precarious balance. Federal-provincial relations may also complicate these factors moreso than in the past since Ontario, Quebec and

Saskatchewan interests differ (as we will see in our case studies).

The relationship between government intervention and foreign and domestic policy determinants can also be seen in current speculation about the Canadian-American connection in nuclear trade relative to our nuclear trade with Europe and Japan, and advanced "third world" countries. Since the adoption of the Trudeau government's so-called "third option" foreign policy[17] in the early-1970s, Canadian foreign policy sought to give more emphasis to obtaining a special contractual relationship with the European community and has been far more conscious of the considerable economic competition of the advanced third world countries and of their desire for access to both energy and advanced technology. It has periodically utilized both reactor sales and/or the strategic value of uranium as instruments of such policy.

While the early evidence may suggest that parts of the "third option" are viable, there are other forces which may be more compelling in the medium and long term and which may lead to a greater continental economic integration with the United States, an integration partly, though not wholly, linked to what might be called, for want of a better phrase, a Canadian-American nuclear equivalent of the auto pact. A Canadian-American energy arrangement is by no means inevitable or even desirable, but it is a distinct possibility. Several factors when combined with the "last chance" technology argument advanced earlier could bring the continental nuclear pact to fruition.

First, future Canadian CANDU reactor sales to third world countries judged to be politically unstable or unacceptable will be subject to intense political criticism. Canadian salesmen may seek out safer terrain among Western states even though earlier efforts in this regard were not successful. Canadian guilt feelings over our loss of international innocence following India's nuclear explosion will reinforce this pressure.

Second, the United States may become a more plausible market for CANDU or partial CANDU sales if the Carter-initiated INFCE study directly or indirectly endorses CANDU-based technology.[18] Because such factors as the current excess capacity in the U.S. nuclear industry, such exports would be marginal in the near future but they could assume larger proportions in the late 1980s and the 1990s.

Third, both Canadian and U.S. official uranium supply and demand "projections" are now quite optimistic. However, it is possible, given the uncertainties of all resource and energy forecasting, that they seriously underestimate the medium term needs of the American nuclear industry (under both pre-INFCE and post-INFCE assumptions). They may also underestimate the probable medium and long term pressures on Canada to reserve part of her uranium supply for her continental neighbour on a preferential basis over others, including other western allies.

Finally, the probabilities of a continental nuclear energy pact will be influenced by tradeoffs in other sectors of Canada-American relations. There is increased pressure, at least on the Canadian side, to utilize the CANDU-uranium question in bargaining over other aspects of Canadian-American trade such as aircraft purchases and resource transactions.

If these factors converged there would be very strong pressure to strike a continental nuclear bargain, with the U.S. benefiting from a reliable and nearby uranium supply and with Canada making just enough CANDU or CANDU-based sales to sustain and perhaps enlarge its high technology nuclear industry. For Canada, the combined practice of "staple" economics and high technology industry development would be a difficult package for decision makers to resist.

That such a future scenario would also present a highly explosive political combination, however, seems obvious. The emotive issue of Canadian-American relations and continental integration would be combined with all the built-in controversy already surrounding the nuclear policy debate. In addition to numerous developments in the U.S. and abroad, as well as the other developments in the Canadian policy process (to be discussed below), the probability of this scenario occurring will be dependent on the evolving domestic pattern of conflict between the pro and anti-nuclear forces. It will also be dependent on many other uncertainties including the reliability of both Canadian and U.S. uranium demand and supply estimates, the possible Canadian need to finance development of the thorium cycle, and the political and economic feasibility of electricity exports of Ontario CANDU-produced electricity to the U.S. The 1979 discussion between Canada and Mexico over oil, CANDUs and uranium suggests that even broader continental energy/economic arrangements are being seriously explored.

(4) Public Sector-Private Sector Relations

The Canadian nuclear industry is dominated by powerful federal and provincial crown corporations including AECL, Eldorado Nuclear, Ontario Hydro, Hydro Quebec, and the New Brunswick Hydro Electric Commission. By comparison, its private sector supply components are dependent and dispersed both as to size and influence. The nuclear industry initially became a state-dominated industry more for security rather than for ideological reasons. It is likely to remain a state-dominated industry for reasons that transcend the initial security rationale and stand in opposition to the recent revival of ideological arguments for cutting back the size of government in general.

We will explore in more detail in our first case study (Chapter 6) precisely how the current public-private mix, especially in the reactor program, evolved. The analysis of the occupational health of uranium miners case (Chapter 7) and the Ontario Hydro uranium contract case (Chapter 8) will show that ideology has, at times, figured more prominently, in decisions of governments to intervene. Thus, an analysis of public sector-private sector relations will be a major focus of the case studies. In an introductory context, however, and especially in relation to the recent climate of public sector-private sector relations, a number of observations can be made.

The Clark Government has announced its intention to sell or "privatize" Eldorado Nuclear Ltd. This was done for reasons unrelated to nuclear policy per se. Rather it was intended to signal and lend some substance to the government's committment to "less government," to control crown corporations and to "return" certain functions to the private sector. Several factors suggest that it is an unlikely candidate for privatization.

First, the recent reorganization of AECL into several profit and corporate centres did not move to the ultimate step of "privatizing."[19] Second, the federal government is unlikely to relinquish direct state control because of its need to deal on a one-to-one basis with provincial public utilities (especially Ontario Hydro) and with numerous directly or indirectly state sponsored investment consortia involved in the recent uranium exploration boom. Numerous investment consortia involve foreign governments either directly or through their public utilities.[20]

The Clark Government's plan to sell Eldorado Nuclear (and parts of Petro Canada) makes little sense. The federal government has only recently secured a direct presence in energy development generally through PetroCan and the tar sands investment. It is strategically unwise to give up either this direct involvement or its involvement in nuclear matters through AECL and Eldorado Nuclear, particularly when it is noted that major oil companies such as Gulf and Imperial Oil are also involved in uranium development.[21] It must be recalled that federal energy authorities were severely criticized in the mid-1970s for having an insufficient knowledge to accurately estimate reserves. Hence they are likely to want a direct role in the industry to give them "a window" on all relevant matters. The current stable of state energy enterprises constitute an important bargaining lever for federal policy-makers with the private sector and with other state-owned parts of the nuclear energy industry. The strategic value of such enterprises would appear to outweigh any incipient conservative ideological benefits. Moreover, the value of Eldorado is reinforced by the continuing security argument, which, though not as strong as in the immediate postwar period, still commands much support.[22]

One effect of a committment to state enterprise in nuclear matters is that advocates of the nuclear option will continue to enjoy a strong role in the policy process. The government itself and the nuclear enterprises it has created have a vested interest in nuclear expansion both for the normal reasons of bureaucratic power, but also because the regulation of the "industry" involves government regulating itself. Again when <u>combined</u> with the arguments advanced earlier about the strategic value of the high technology nuclear industry, the state enterprise variable assumes a special political importance.

(5) <u>Federal-Provincial Relations</u>

As our analysis of the policy process in Chapter 4 will make clear, nuclear policy and intervention choices are increasingly influenced by federal-provincial bargaining. Although the federal government has ways of influencing policy in all energy and resources sectors, it is to be remembered that nuclear power and uranium are virtually the only resource policy areas where primary authority is in federal rather than in provincial government hands. Thus in recent federal-provincial constitutional bargaining, where decentralization pressures arising from the Quebec separatists and western economic challenge are strong, the federal government is under pressure to, but is unlikely to want to, trade away or dissipate its one direct resource bargaining lever.

The proposed, but not implemented, <u>Nuclear Control and Administration Act</u> (Bill C-14, introduced on November 24, 1977) and the political timidity in carrying it forward to its legislative conclusion are perhaps belated reflections of the fact that the federal government is reluctant to give away too much. Federal jurisdiction in the existing <u>Atomic Energy Control Act</u> was largely claimed on grounds of security and in relation to federal powers over declared undertakings of general benefit to Canada. Bill C-14, however, far more explicitly embraced health and environmental grounds for federal involvement, as well as the security grounds, and hence invited greater provincial opposition politically if not legally.

Such opposition has already been reflected in criticism by the Western provinces:

> The western provinces reaffirm the concerns expressed by the provinces at the Provincial Deputy Minister of Mines Meeting, January 19, 1978. They consider the federal-provincial consultations which occurred prior to the introduction of Bill C-14 in the House of Commons to have been inadequate since the federal government did not indicate to the provinces the full scope of the proposed legislation. The provinces point out that Part I duplicates provincial, as well as, federal health and environmental legislation. They indicate grave concerns with regard to Section 63 which empowers the Minister of Energy, Mines and Resources to control the sale, lease, management, exploration, mining, and expropriation of nuclear resources. The provinces recognize that the federal government has special interests with regard to nuclear resources. They feel, however, that aspects of this new policy are a direct encroachment by the federal government into provincial jurisdiction over the control and management of natural resources. The provinces maintain that Section 63 of Bill C-14 should be deleted, or at the very least, should not be proclaimed until the provinces have become convinced of its necessity. The western provinces also seek clarification of the new Nuclear Control Board's activities and the composition of the Board's membership.[23]

In addition, Ontario has expressed concern about the broader public hearing processes envisaged by the new bill. It is to be remembered, moreover, that the new legislation was initially spawned in response to the 1975-76 concern about the Port Hope and uranium miners controversies (see Chapter 7), but it entered the parliamentary process in 1977 when constitutional and economic matters were more visible, and more urgent. Although, as we will see, there are many good reasons for the bill being adopted, its slow progress (and perhaps its future demise or emasculation) may be due to a belated federal reluctance to risk giving up an important source of resource and constitutional bargaining leverage.

There is a sense in which the two kinds of leverage (public-private and federal-provincial) described in this and the last section may reinforce each other, giving the nuclear interest in _federal_ policy processes a degree of political clout they would not otherwise enjoy. Corresponding "non-nuclear" or "limited nuclear" interests may thus be weaker. This is a fact of considerable importance since nuclear policy and energy policy outcomes will be significantly influenced in the future by the institutional nature and outcomes of bargaining among departments and agencies with major roles in the nuclear field, a subject on which Chapter 4 will focus.

NOTES: Chapter 3

1. See, for example, Harold A. Innis, _Essays in Canadian Economic History_ (Toronto: University of Toronto Press, 1956).

2. For recent general analyses of these interrelated aspects, see Richard W. Phidd and G. Bruce Doern, _The Politics and Management of Canadian Economic Policy_ (Toronto: Macmillan of Canada, 1978); Senate Standing Committee on Foreign Affairs, _Canada-United States Trade Relations_, Vol. 11, (Ottawa: Minister of Supply and Services Canada, 1978); "What will save troubled manufacturing," _Financial Post_, December 17, 1977, pp. 36-38; and Conference Board of Canada, _Canada's Manufacturing Sector: Performance in the 1970s_ (Ottawa, 1978).

3. On the Arrow and related aspect of industrial/ technology policies see James Dow, The Arrow (Toronto: Lorimer and Co., 1979); D. Middlemiss, "The Political Economy of Defence: Dimensions of Government Involvement in the Canadian Aircraft Industry," Paper given to Canadian Political Science Association Meetings, London, Ontario, May 29, 1978; and M. Skinner "The Federal Make or Buy R & D Policy: A Preliminary Evaluation of Policy and Implementation." Unpublished M.A. thesis, School of Public Administration, Carleton University, 1978.

4. See John N.H. Britton and James M. Gilmour, The Weakest Link: A Technological Perspective on Canadian Industrial Underdevelopment. (Ottawa: Science Council of Canada, 1978), Science Council of Canada, Forging the Links (Ottawa: Minister of Supply and Services Canada, 1979) and Andrew H. Wilson, Government and Innovation (Ottawa: Information Canada, 1973).

5. G. Bruce Doern, The Atomic Energy Control Board. (Ottawa: Law Reform Commission of Canada, 1977).

6. Gordon Sims, "The Evolution of AECL." Unpublished M.A. thesis, Institute of Canadian Studies, Carleton University, Ottawa, 1979.

7. See David Pearce, G. Beuret and L. Edwards, "Opposition to Civilian Nuclear Power and the Role of the Public Enquiry," Paper prepared for Annual Conference on Uranium Supply and Demand, London, Uranium Institute, July 10-12, 1978; and Nigel Hawkins, "Science in Europe: The Antinuclear Movement Takes Hold," Science, September 16, 1977, pp. 1167-1168.

8. For a range of views on the evolving Canadian nuclear debate, see Alan Wyatt, The Nuclear Challenge: Understanding the Debate (Toronto: Book Press, 1978); Charles Law and Ron Glen, Critical Choice: Nuclear Power in Canada (Toronto: Corpus, 1978); and F. Knelman, Nuclear Energy - The

Unforgiving Technology (Edmonton: Hurtig Publishers, 1976).

9. B. Toller, "Public Attitudes to Nuclear Power," Unpublished Research Paper, School of Public Administration, Carleton University, Ottawa, 1978.

10. Interviews by the author. For U.S. poll data in Three Mile Island see Marc A. Schulman, "The Impact of Three Mile Island," *Public Opinion*, Vol. 2, No. 3, June/ July 1979, pp. 7-13.

11. See Michael D. Ornstein, *Canadian Policy Makers' Views on Nuclear Energy* (Toronto: York University Institute for Behavioural Research, November 1976); J.K. Dobson, B. Greer-Wooten, L. Mitson, *National Assessment of Public Perceptions and Attitudes to Nuclear Power in Canada*. Canadian Nuclear Association Conference Papers, June 13-16, 1976, Vol. 3, pp. 32-105.

12. See G. Bruce Doern, *Science and Politics in Canada* (Montreal: McGill-Queen's University Press, 1972).

13. G. Bruce Doern, *The Atomic Energy Control Board* op. cit.

14. See for example N.M. Ediger, "Notes for a Paper on the Nuclear Controversy in Canada." The Uranium Institute International Symposium on Uranium Supply and Demand, London, England, July 10-12, 1978; Robert G. Rosehart, "Towards More Productive Public Participation," paper prepared for Annual Meeting of the Canadian Nuclear Association, Ottawa, June 1978.

15. See R. Morrison and E. Wonder, "Canada's Nuclear Export Policy" in G. Bruce Doern and R. Morrison (eds.) *Canadian Nuclear Policies* (Montreal: Instutute for Research on Public Policy, 1980), Chapter 4; Albert Legault, "Nuclear Policy and Canadian Foreign Policy" in Doern and Morrison, *op. cit.*, Chapter 6; and Steven J. Warnecke, "Fuel Assurance and Supply Security," International Sym-

posium on Uranium Supply and Demand, London, July 10-12, 1978.

16. See, for example, J.J. Shepherd, "We Must Have Industrial Policy or Stay Third Rate," <u>Globe and Mail</u>, October 2, 1978, p. 7.

17. See Bruce Thordarson, <u>Trudeau and Foreign Policy</u> (Toronto: Oxford University Press, 1972).

18. A similar scenario of closer U.S.-Canada ties is suggested as a reasonable possibility in a recent analysis, see Hugh C. McIntyre, <u>Uranium, Nuclear Power and Canada-U.S. Energy Relations</u> (Montreal: C.D. Howe Research Institute, 1978).

19. AECL, News Release, July 28, 1978.

20. Department of Energy, Mines and Resources, <u>Brief to the Cluff Lake Board of Inquiry</u> (Regina, Saskatchewan, April 1977).

21. For a survey of major oil company investment in mining (including uranium), see <u>The Economist</u>, September 16, 1978, pp. 82-84.

22. The election of a Progressive Conservative Government critical of Petro Canada does not alter this personal prediction. The new government will be under enormous pressure to retain its energy enterprise as an important instrument of policy.

23. <u>Report of the Western Premiers' Task Force on Constitutional Trends</u>, Second Report, April 1978, p. 46.

Chapter 4

Science, Technology and Nuclear Policy

The degree of world media attention which was focussed on the Three Mile Island reactor accident in the United States in the spring of 1979 demonstrated clearly how nuclear power has become the symbol of intense political and social concern about the management and desirability of large scale technological projects especially those whose potential hazards must be assessed in relation to geological rather than man-made concepts of time. Intervention in the nuclear industry is clearly the product of a number of factors related to the role of science and technology. Previous chapters have already alluded to important technological dimensions including the early faith in technology which propelled the development of CANDU, the alleged importance of high technology industries to Canadian economic development, the importance of technological change in fuel enrichment and in advanced breeder reactors, and the contrasting values held about science and scientists revealed in the positions taken by pro and anti-nuclear interest groups.

These are without doubt important elements in the nuclear debate and we will examine them again in relation to the case studies. There are, however, other more particular aspects of the role of science and technology which effect intervention and which must be examined in some detail if nuclear policy decisions and non-decisions are to be understood.

These aspects include Hafele's concept of "hypotheticality" in the nuclear power debate[1]; the openness of the regulatory process; the relationships between causal knowledge and political perception; the relationship between the research priorities and the lack of applied controls and monitoring technology; the degree of deference paid by domestic regulators to international standard-setting bodies; and finally the redistributive effects encouraged by a lack of appropriate science and technology priorities.

Nuclear policy is affected by the full spectrum of scientific and technological activity including the acquisition, analysis and publication of data, the pursuit of pure research (or the search for causal knowledge), the adoption and adaptation of applied production technologies, and the development and deployment of applied technologies (for example, to monitor exposure in the workplace). It is therefore affected by the timely availability of scientific and technological personnel, and by the way in which new research is received and communicated by regulators, policy-makers and their advisors.

(1) Hypotheticality

In the general realm of the relations between science and government, nuclear power properly deserves a unique set of characterizations. Hafele's effort to relate the nulcear controversy to the politics of hypotheticality is indicative of such characterizations. He points out that:

> Hypotheticality, of course, is not a word in regular usage but its logic expresses precisely what must be expressed in the line of reasoning presented here. Its logic is the same as that of the word "criticality," for example a term which is familiar to reactor engineers. The rule followed is that for Latin words ending in -itas, for example, veritas or felicitas. Such substantives point to features which exist in principle and which if actualized, lead to the fact that something can have a certain property: a reactor can become critical or a situation can be considered to be hypothetical. The process of interaction between theory and experiment which leads to truth in its traditional sense is no longer possible. Such truth can no longer be fully experienced.

> This means that arguments in the hypothetical domain necessarily and ultimately remain inconclusive. I think that this ultimate inconclusiveness which is inherent in our task explains, to some extent, the peculiarities of the public debate on nuclear reactor safety. The strange and often unreal features of that debate, in my judgment, are connected with the "hypotheticality" of the domain below the level of the residual risk.[2]

Thus, standards of proof, and risk-benefit calculations, cannot easily or reassuringly be offered. The technological mystery of several aspects of the nuclear regulatory process cannot be underestimated. It affects both <u>substantive</u> standards and how they are perceived. For example, some judge the nuclear alternative to be too risky and thus seek its abolition. Others wish to be more convincingly reassured. These standards in turn impose different criteria regarding the adequacy of nuclear policy objectives and processes.

Important parts of the nuclear regulatory debate are conducted in the realm of hypotheticality in that the more typical standards of demonstrable proof often cannot be achieved. Questions of nuclear reactor breakdowns, nuclear disasters, and waste storage in geologically-safe, underground caves are issues which, in more than most, take both the regulators and the public into the indeterminable arena of hypothetical standards.

(2) <u>The Openness of the Regulatory Process</u>

The role of science and technology and the openness of the nuclear regulatory process are intricately linked. This link can be seen in relation to the two competing models of regulation about which Canadian regulators tend to generalize, as well as in relation to the question of which organizations should properly conduct research in support of the regulatory function.[3] It also affects the rate and timing of the adoption of production and safety technology by the industries being regulated.

Many people directly involved in the Canadian nuclear regulatory process, implicitly or explicitly, have two polar regulatory models in mind. As a shorthand I will call these models the professionally open model (Model 1) and the democratic open model (Model 2).

Model 1, the professionally open model, is a model of regulation characterized by a high degree of mutual trust. Its proponents assert that it is <u>internally</u> open in that it fosters frank criticism and evaluation <u>among</u> professional technical people. Thus its advocates suggest that when regulators arrive, under Model 1, the industries are likely to view them as professional people trying to achieve a common goal — for example, health and safety. Professionals in the industry are more likely to show their professional peers both things that are working well, and areas where difficulties are present. Thus an internally open (to professionals) and frank process of evaluation will, it is argued by some, promote effective regulation by experts who know what the problems are. Model 1 will also be characterized by minimum reporting requirements and fewer hearings, thus giving the "front-line" regulators (the professionals in the industry) more time to spend on "real" health and safety public interest issues. In other words, it is claimed that less time would be spent "pushing paper" to the regulatory board merely to comply with formal requirements, and more spent in improving real health and safety.

Model 2 is based implicitly, if not explicitly, on the American model, in which the processes would be more democratically open. Extensive hearing procedures would be required and opportunities for litigation by interested groups would be broadened. As a consequence, Model 2's opponents claim that the processes would induce a damaging environment of confrontation. Regulatory professionals would be viewed by "the regulated" much more in an "us versus them" adversarial fashion. In day-to-day regulatory and compliance relationships regulators would more likely be given only exactly the information they ask for, rather than take part in a frank discussion of problems. The procedural requirements of Model 2 would necessitate much more time being spent by the regulated in complying with the formal requirements of regulation.

Both models represent over-simplifications, but they do reflect differences in relative costs and benefits which have to be frankly taken into account. This study reflects a view in which regulatory reform is seen as moving towards Model 2. There has been too much professional "coziness." The evolution towards Model 2, however, should not be seen as being achievable without costs. The democratically closed, but professionally open, model which Canada has tended to adopt has probably had some benefits. For example, Canada's stringent requirements in <u>some</u> aspects of possible reactor breakdown may be partly attributable to the close professional contact. The less onerous paper work and hearings processes have left industry professionals more time to deal with substantive problems of health and safety.

It is also true, however, that there is a very fine line between professionally open and frank exchanges, and professional coziness. Both the <u>substance</u> and <u>appearance</u> of professional coziness become all the more critical the more one is dealing with a technologically complex and scientifically mysterious area of regulation. All regulatory areas have some degree of technological complexity, but some have a great deal more than others. The regulation of broadcasting and the regulation of atomic energy, for example, will have many similar procedural issues. However, <u>in degree</u>, the regulation of nuclear energy is characterized by much greater technological difficulty as far as laymen's understanding and control are concerned. It is this degree of difference which imposes extra obligations on nuclear regulatory authorities to establish greater independence and to create more open regulatory and compliance processes to facilitate better public understanding and to promote real health and safety.

The degree of openness is influenced by the issue of the independence and/or the <u>appearance</u> of independence of the research associated with the activities being regulated, and the freedom or ease with which the knowledge is traded and communicated. Scientists tend to think of research as a search for causal knowledge and secondarily as an input to government and other decision-making processes. This characterization of research is frequently accurate. Research, however, is also an output and a political and economic weapon. One frequently duplicates research precisely because one agency distrusts, or cannot be <u>seen</u> to be excessively trusting and deferring to research done by others. To study a problem or to seek more knowledge is frequently a middle of the road alternative between doing nothing and taking more vigorous action.

While the call for more research can frequently be nothing more than a cover for inaction, one cannot dispute the fact that in some areas of nuclear energy much research is needed (for example research on mine tailings and on long term exposure to low levels of radiation). An understanding of the research role in the nuclear policy process must therefore include the broad policies and practices which affect research funding. Of these policies and practices three seem to be especially germane: the so-called "little science" pattern of funding through granting bodies; the relationship between in-house research, the federal "make or buy" policy and the regulatory function; and the extent to which such research is freely exchanged with the affected public groups.

The pattern of "little science" funding through the major granting councils is basically a passive "bottom-up" form of research funding.[4] It exists primarily to support good researchers and, through group assessment, to further the frontiers of applied and basic knowledge. In this arena of government-funded university-based research, the emergence of research on issues of occupational health is dependent upon individual initiatives by researchers. While discussions have been held in recent years to give a possible "aggressive" or active role to granting bodies to encourage research in areas where gaps exist the granting councils have not encouraged this idea. Occupational and environmental health is also an area where the borderline or grey areas between medical research, regular scientific research, nuclear research (AECB) and social science may be especially hard to deal with. While individual research proposals on occupational health are funded through this system the funding is intermittent, the skills of grantsmanship of a high entrepreneurial order are required. All of the above has been severely affected by the drastic cuts in the rate of growth of recent federal science budgets.[5]

Another possible area of funding is the so-called mission-oriented research and development funded by departments or carried out by departments in their own laboratories. The intent of federal policy, under the umbrella of the "make or buy" contracting-out policy, has been to reverse the historic pattern of domination by in-house government research, and to have more research carried on outside of government, particularly by industry. The policy puts the onus on federal agencies to automatically contract out their research needs unless they can provide specific justification for doing it internally. Among the possible justifications for doing the research in house are security, or if the research is in direct support of a regulatory function.

The latter was mysteriously viewed by the drafters of the "make or buy" policy as being a rationale that could be used only in "exceptional" circumstances.[6] The nuclear and related occupational health fields illustrate how unexceptional this exception is. Research in support of regulation should not in principal be contracted out to the industry being regulated. In practice this is a difficult principle to apply in some areas. What it does suggest, however, is that the research must then be done in-house or be contracted out to universities or other research establishments that are sufficiently, and are <u>perceived to be</u> sufficiently, independent, and which openly communicate their findings.

The openness of the regulatory process is ultimately constrained by the problems of the transfer of production technology between or among regulated firms in the industry. Part of a corporation's response to the suggestion of building better and safer production processes is influenced by the question of sunk capital costs and commitment to existing technology.[7] A corporation is reluctant to invest new capital when it will only yield new costs rather than additional benefits. Thus the standard response in matters concerning new safety technology is either to say that there is no proven causal link between the hazard and the occupational condition or that the new technology does not exist to comply with suggested new standards or that it cannot be done for several years or months. In some instances a time lag is clearly necessary. In others, time is merely another way of expressing the higher priority to be accorded capital as opposed to labour (or other bearers of the costs of less superior safety production technologies).

Obstacles clearly exist in the free transfer of production technology from one firm to another, both within the industry and where applicable from the multinational parent to its branch plant. While almost all industrial spokesmen argue that the uranium industry should use the "best available technology" in the industry, the fact remains that there are severe constraints in the transfer of this technology from firm to firm because safety technology is tied to trade secrets, to different mining concepts, and to pre-existing investments of each firm. There is a clear divergence between private and social efficiency under such conditions.

It is important to stress the extent to which the regulation of such areas as uranium mining is also tied to the company town. Elliot Lake and other mining communities are synonomous with the concept of resource-based, hinterland-located company towns. One industry is the economic life blood of the area. This imposes further constraints on the openness and visibility of regulation. The remoteness of many of these communities from provincial and federal capitals, and hence from regulators, makes them easier to ignore (and harder to regulate).

(3) Causal Knowledge and Political Perceptions

Government intervention is profoundly affected by the different views about the existence of causal knowledge possessed by scientists on the one hand, and by workers or others directly affected by the regulatory process on the other. Scientists, for example, are naturally and necessarily cautious about the statements they make about causal knowledge. They have a more cautious sense of what constitutes "evidence" to establish standards or TLV's (threshold limit values), for example. They are likely to advocate, therefore, that the standards be viewed as guidelines and that more research be done. Economic interests that stand to gain by loose standards will exploit this argument and use it to justify looser standards or to postpone action until more conclusive "cause and effect" evidence is produced. Unions and others who must seek more precise administrative and legal criteria of evidence will opt for precise standards embodied in legislation (or regulations) and will point to a number of cases where occupational disability or death has occurred.

The history of occupational health in general, and the health of uranium miners in particular, bears witness to the constant presence of two levels of experience about causal knowledge and evidence.[8] One form is found in the more rarified level of scientific journals and symposia. A second is found in union halls and work sites or workmen's compensation cases. The first type of experience tends to view the second as being merely a series of "cases" and hence not causal evidence. The second type of experience tends to perceive the first to be remote, foreign and largely subservient to interests other than its own. The bridging of the gap between the two, each of which ought to have a compelling claim to legitimacy, is a major problem to be overcome in the regulatory process, since it affects the burden of proof and who must bear it. The ignorance of each other's world on the part of the custodian of each of these kinds of experience is enormous, and as we will see in Chapter 7, is vividly reflected in the regulation of the health of Canadian uranium miners.

(4) Science and Technology Priorities: The Mix of Basic and Applied Research

Regulators need both basic research and applied technology to do their job well. They also have to arrange for or otherwise ensure that there are qualified scientific personnel to carry out the work needed now or in the future. As we have noted in the previous discussion of research funding, this capacity to plan for scientific and technological needs is usually not within the regulatory authority's exclusive domain. The uranium miners' case shows that research to generate causal knowledge is not the only "scientific" dimension of the nuclear regulatory process. Equally important is the development of technology that can make regulatory objectives achievable in practice. Technology to measure radiation exposure in the mine work areas and in the development of superior ventilation equipment are essential to practical day-to-day regulatory compliance. So also is the technology of epidemiological studies and related medical record linkages.[9]

Public policy, administration and research on technology are intricately connected in the nuclear policy process. The research priorities of Canadian nuclear regulatory authorities historically have focused on basic nuclear physics. They have left the development of control technology to the nuclear power industry and to the uranium mining companies, thus contributing greatly to an excessive dependence on private firms for information with which to regulate the industry.

(5) Deference to International Standard-Setting Bodies

Canadian nuclear regulatory authorities utilize the knowledge, expertise and other experience of international and foreign organizations involved in nuclear energy and occupational and environmental health. Bodies like the International Committee on Radiological Protection (ICRP) and the American Conference of Governmental Industrial Hygienists (ACGIH) are invaluable sources of expertise and advice. Canadian involvement with other international research and advisory bodies such as the International Labour Organization, the World Health Organization, the Organization for European Cooperation and Development, and the International Atomic Energy Agency are also immensely valuable. Canadian agencies have also benefited from close day-to-day professional contacts and exchange with their counterparts in the United States and in other countries, particularly the Nuclear Regulatory Commission, the National Institute of Occupational Safety and Health (NIOSH) and the Occupational Safety and Health Administration (OSHA). The considerably greater American resources and Canada's proximity to the United States thus confer a considerable advantage.

While no one would argue that these total international and foreign resources should not be utilized, it is also important to point out the dangers that can occur if Canadian regulatory authorities depend excessively on them. It is easy for a sense of deference to an international peer group to exist. Standards developed in an international arena are frequently subject to the wider trade-offs and compromises that may develop not only out of scientific controversy but also out of the differing views of producer and consumer countries. On the other hand it is also frequently the case that regulators will fail to utilize international research findings of direct regulatory relevance. Worse still, as Chapter 7 will show, they fail even to inform those most affected by the research, namely workers and their labour unions, about the meaning and possible impact of the research that is available.

(6) Science, Technology and Redistribution

The case study on Canadian uranium miners (Chapter 7) will show that the choices about science and technology have profound redistributive effects on different economic classes and groups. The costs of regulation, and the failure to pursue certain kinds of research, fall disproportionately on certain groups. Just as the nuclear research community has difficulty responding to single cases in the context of its search for causal knowledge, so too does it have difficulty with relatively small sub-populations, especially those such as uranium mine workers who are geographically isolated in remote mining communities. It might be expected that social science research would shed light on these redistributive consequences, but this has not generally been the case. In the Canadian case it has been direct political criticism and action, rather than research, that has pinpointed the redistributive consequences of past research and regulatory behaviour. It should be stressed that not all nuclear workers, or workers affected by radiation, have been ignored. Workers in nuclear power plants, and X-ray technicians and other hospital workers, have received much more attention. This may be the case because they work in the middle range of the nuclear fuel cycle where regulatory priorities have been placed and because they are white-collar technical workers scattered through larger urban communities.

NOTES: Chapter 4

1. W. Hafele, "Hypotheticality and the New Challenge: The Path Finder Role of Nuclear Policy," Minerva, Vol. 12, 1974, p. 314.

2. Ibid., pp. 314-315.

3. For a broader analysis see the papers in G. Bruce Doern (ed.) The Regulatory Process in Canada (Toronto: Macmillan of Canada, 1978).

4. See G. Bruce Doern, Science and Politics in Canada (Montreal: McGill-Queen's Press, 1972).

5. P. Meyboom, "In House vs Contractual Research," Canadian Public Administration, Vol. 17, No. 4 (Winter 1974), pp. 563-585. See also The Make or

<u>Buy Policy, 1973-1975</u> (Ottawa: Ministry of State for Science and Technology, November 1975).

6. Mel Skinner, "The Federal Make or Buy Policy: A Preliminary Evaluation of Policy and Implementation." Unpublished M.A. thesis, School of Public Administration, Carleton University, Ottawa, 1978.

7. Roger Noll, <u>Reforming Regulation</u> (Washington: Brookings Institution, 1971), pp. 25-26.

8. This is the constant factor in the cases analysed in Paul Brodeur, <u>Expendable Americans</u> (New York: The Viking Press, 1973); and Rachel Scott, <u>Muscle and Blood</u> (New York: E.P. Dutton & Co., 1974). It is also found in the six case studies analysed in G. Bruce Doern, <u>Regulatory Processes and Jurisdictional Issues in Regulating Hazardous Substances</u> (Ottawa: Science Council of Canada, 1977), Chapters 3, 4 and 5. More generally, see G.B. Reschenthaler, <u>Occupational Health and Safety in Canada: The Economics and Three Case Studies</u> (Montreal: Institute for Research on Public Policy, 1979).

9. <u>Report of the Royal Commisson on the Health and Safety of Workers in Mines</u>. (Toronto: Ontario Queen's Printer, 1976).

Chapter 5

Organization, Process and Policy

The three case studies examined in subsequent chapters span events in the 1950s, 1960s and 1970s. It is necessary, therefore, to have a general appreciation of the evolution of federal and provincial nuclear policy organization and processes during this period, a task to which the first part of this chapter is devoted.[1] It is also essential to describe the central statutory and nonstatutory policies which have gradually been put in place since the dawning of the nuclear age in Canada. We will leave the detailed analysis of the ways in which these organizations, processes and policies have influenced intervention decisions to later chapters.

In reviewing nuclear policy, organization and processes it is useful to distinguish the promotional from the control aspects of nuclear intervention. Promotion is exercised through public expenditures and grants, loans, tax policy, as well as through publicity, speeches and behind the scenes negotiations. Control is exercised through the making of regulations and the prescribing of standards, the issuing of permits and licenses, and the development and operation of inspection, monitoring and compliance procedures to ensure that standards of health, safety and security are adhered to. Inevitably these promotion and control processes involve action by serval federal and provincial departments and agencies. As such they invite problems of intergovernmental and inter-agency coordination, cooperation, and conflict. In the case of uranium mining, for example, such federal agencies as the Atomic Energy Control Board, the departments of National Health and Welfare; Energy, Mines and Resources; Environment; Industry, Trade and Commerce; External Affairs; and Transport, among others, are involved. At the provincial level such departments as

Environment, Health, Labour, Mineral Resources, and Northern Development are involved.

More specifically, the control process involves exploration permits, licenses for siting, constructing, operating and decommissioning the mining, milling or reactor facilities, licenses for waste disposal and for transportation of prescribed substances, licenses for inspectors, and permits for exports.

(1) Organization and Process: Towards Pluralization?

Although the time periods are somewhat arbitrary it is nonetheless useful to differentiate two phases in the evolution of the nuclear policy process. These periods are 1945 to the late 1960s and 1970 to the present. The former largely comprises the period when nuclear policy was the almost exclusive product of relatively private behind the scenes discussions dominated by officials and experts. The recent period has been characterized by a large number of policy participants, greater attention by elected politicians, interest groups, and the media and high intergovernmental and international stakes.

Figures 5.1 and 5.2 attempt to portray these different periods, albeit in a static fashion. The case studies will add some flesh to these bones and joints of the nuclear policy process. As Figure 5.1 indicates, the early policy process nominally involved a number of agencies but was largely a product of close interaction between senior officials of AECL, Ontario Hydro, and key federal and Ontario Ministers. The existence at the federal level of an interdepartmental panel on atomic energy was more form than substance. Lorne Gray, President of AECL from 1958 to 1976, virtually ignored the committee and instead cultivated relationships with a few key officials in the central agencies of the federal government.[2] At the same time, as our first case study will show, Ontario Hydro enjoyed considerable independence both from the Ontario Cabinet and the Ontario Legislature. The heart of the nuclear policy process was an AECL-Ontario Hydro alliance nurtured in the 1950s. Our

- 69 -

Figure 5.1
MAJOR NUCLEAR POLICY ORGANIZATIONS 1945 TO LATE 1960s

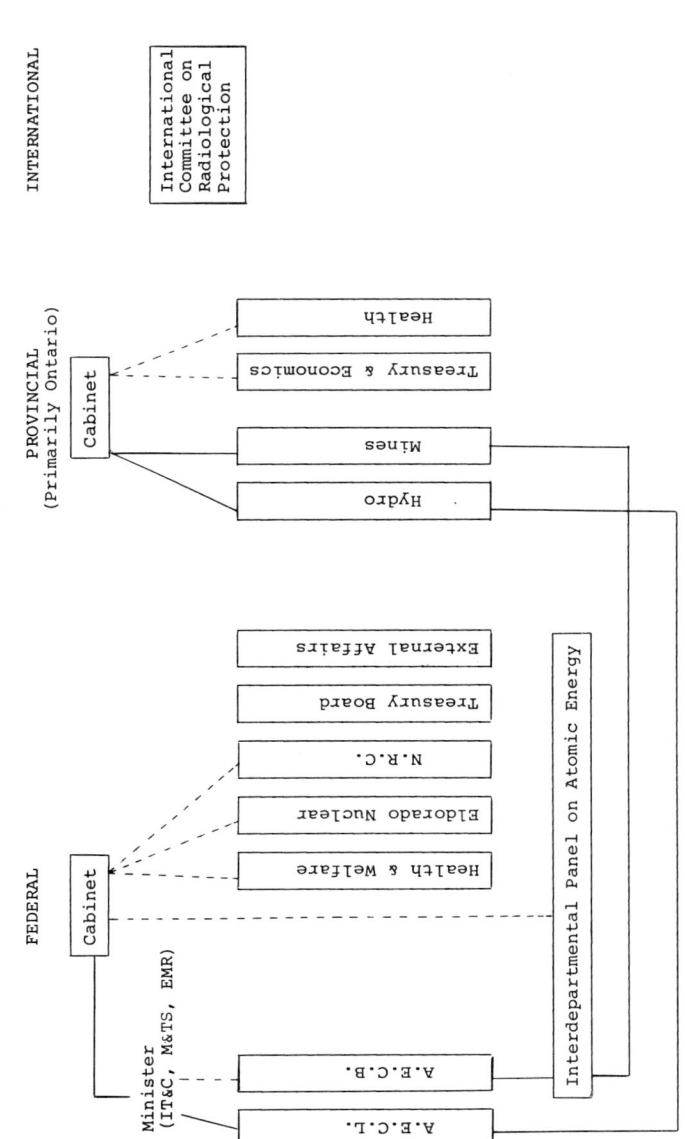

– 70 –

Figure 5.2

MAJOR NUCLEAR POLICY ORGANIZATIONS 1970 TO PRESENT

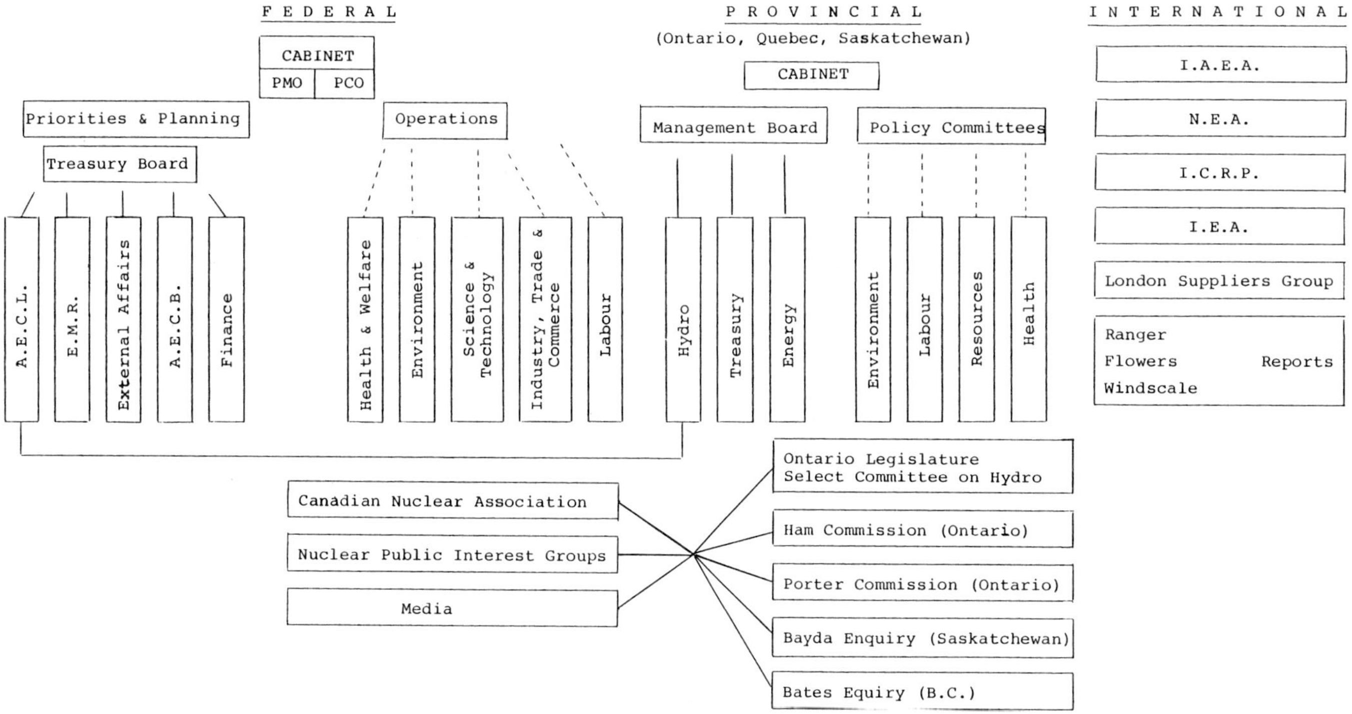

second case study on uranium mining (Chapter 8) will show, however, that a second level alliance or accommodation was also struck between the Atomic Energy Control Board (AECB) and provincial mines and health departments.

Internal federal policy processes were largely dominated by AECL as the Department of Energy, Mines and Resources (EMR) had but limited expertise and nuclear issues were only beginning to arouse controversy. Other agencies like the AECB and Eldorado Nuclear were more passive bystanders, although not unimportant in their own spheres of activity. In the 1970s, as Figure 5.2 shows, domestic health and safety issues and foreign policy concerns reached a new, and above all, visible level of importance and thus departments and agencies such as the AECB, External Affairs, EMR, and National Health and Welfare began to seek and partially obtain greater influence. The Treasury Board, Privy Council Office and the Department of Finance also became more involved as the political controversy and the economic importance of nuclear questions increased. The influence of the latter was also a product of the general strengthening of the role of central agencies and cabinet committees by the Trudeau government.[3]

In the 1970s at the provincial level, especially in Ontario and Quebec, the policy process also came to include a larger number of departments and agencies. In both provinces energy ministries were created in large measure to reduce the policy dominance of their hydro utilities. Figure 5.2 also indicates the growing influence of the media, the strengthened presence of more formal interest groups on both sides of the nuclear question and the influence of several commissions and enquiries on nuclear matters. By the 1970s the number of international agencies and organizations directly or indirectly involved had increased markedly and now included not only the ICRP but also the International Atomic Energy Agency (given new impetus by the signing of the Non-Proliferation Treaty), the Nuclear Energy Agency (NEA) sponsored by the OECD, the International Energy Agency (IEA) created to respond to the Arab Oil Embargo of 1973, and the London Suppliers Group, created in 1976 by nuclear suppliers to agree on stricter safeguards for international nuclear trade. Several nuclear enquiries in other countries also had some influence in Canada, particularly the Flowers and Windscale enquiries in the U.K. and the Ranger enquiry in Australia.[4] The nuclear debate in the United States became increasingly public and influenced Canadian public opinion, particularly after the combined effect of the accident at Three Mile Island in 1979, and later the Ontario Legislature Hearings.[5]

At first glance one may be tempted to conclude that nuclear policy processes in Canada are now more pluralistic and competitive than they used to be. To a certain extent this pluralism was reflected in the negotiations that accompanied the drafting of the proposed 1977 federal <u>Nuclear Control and Administration Act</u> (Bill C-14). The Bill arose initially from a concern within the AECB that its mandate would have to be altered and its role made more open and independent. This initiative went nowhere until a direct intervention by the PCO resulted in the creation of an interagency committee headed by Maurice LeClair, then Secretary to the Ministry of State for Science and Technology. The division of the subsequent Bill into Part I and II was a direct reflection of the differences of view present in the LeClair Committee and which continued into the later stages of Legislative drafting. Indeed these differences continue to this day.

Part I of the Bill reflects the desire to secure a more independent and open regulatory apparatus. It does not, however, represent the views of anti-nuclear advocates, but rather the view of those who feel that the nuclear option is here to stay and that it must be managed and regulated more openly in the public interest. Part II of Bill C-14 reflects the promotional side of the nuclear equation, but it also contains sections which have generated some provincial concerns that the "feds" may be contemplating some future form of domestic price regulation of uranium. The fact that the two parts of the Bill will be assigned to different ministers also suggests greater pluralization of policy making.

While parts of the Bill represent genuine and needed reform and reflect a fair amount of internal policy competition, one must still be conscious of longer term forces which make policy pluralism more illusory than real. First, the monopoly of expertise still rests with AECL and the provincial utilities, especially Ontario Hydro. Second, the effective implementation of Part I of Bill C-14 depends on the commitment of new regulatory and research resources by the Treasury Board, a commitment whose strength could be sapped by general commitment to cut down on regulation of the economy generally.[6] In this sense the nuclear regulatory baby may be thrown out with the anti-regulatory bath water. Third, the growing concern about the economy is likely to result in intense interest by the Finance Department and the PCO about the economic value of nuclear power and uranium in the face of international economic competition. Thus, although an increase in policy pluralism can be seen there is still none the less an internal community of interest within the federal government favoring nuclear power. It is not necessarily stridently pro-nuclear, but it is a community which sees the need to manage this technological and economic asset more sensibly.

(2) <u>Federal Statutory and Policy Arrangements</u>

The <u>British North America Act</u> of 1867, through a 1930 amendment, conferred the ownership and control of resources on the provinces. Uranium and nuclear matters became the exception to this division of powers, with the passage of the <u>Atomic Energy Control Act</u> in 1946. The Act was based on Section 92-10(c) of the <u>BNA Act</u> which allows the Parliament of Canada to declare a "local work and undertaking" to be "for the general advantage of Canada."[7] Thus formal regulatory authority resides with the federal Atomic Energy Control Board (AECB). Politically, and practically, however, regulation has required provincial cooperation due to the provinces' responsibility under the <u>BNA Act</u> for health, labour and mineral resources.

(a) The Atomic Energy Control Act

The primary role of the AECB is set out in the Atomic Energy Control Act 1946 (S.C. 1946, Chapter 37 - now the Atomic Energy Control Act R.S.C., 1952, Chapter 11 as amended) and is influenced by other policy statements (non-statutory) such as those on Uranium Policy and Safeguards Policy, by several related federal statutes and regulations such as transportation regulation, and by some provincial statutes and practices.[8]

The Atomic Energy Control Act authorized the AECB to control atomic energy materials and equipment in the interests of safety and physical security, to control atomic energy materials, equipment and information in the interests of national and international security, to award grants in aid of atomic energy research, and finally to administer certain aspects of the Nuclear Liability Act (enacted in 1976).

The Atomic Energy Control Act confers on the AECB and on the Cabinet a great array of control powers including the power to regulated, to license, to revoke or suspend licenses, to expropriate, to create crown enterprises, to require the submission of information and reports and to give grants for research and development. Although no statutory provisions for hearings are required the Bill C-14 (Nuclear Control and Administration Act) introduced in 1977 contains a requirement for such hearings.[9]

The constitutional validity of the Atomic Energy Control Act was tested in Pronto Uranium Mines Ltd. vs. Ontario Labour Relations Board, (1956) O.R. 562, and reaffirmed in 1972 by the Ontario High Court in Denision Mines Ltd. vs. Attorney General of Canada, (1972) 32 D.L.R. 419. While the formal constitutional authority seems clear, the AECB has tread carefully in areas where health beyond the immediate perimeters of the nuclear facility are concerned, and in fields such as uranium mining where its power run into aspects of provincial jurisdiction over health and resources. In general terms, however, the AECB and the federal Cabinet can be said to be well armed with a wide array of powers.

(b) The Atomic Energy Control Regulations

The AECB exercises control through its Atomic Energy Control Regulations (P.C. 1974-1195, 30 May, 1974), which include a comprehensive licensing system.[10] Strategic or security controls are exercised over a number of prescribed substances and strategic materials (e.g., uranium, plutonium, thorium, heavy water) and equipment through a permit system operated with the cooperation of the Departments of Industry, Trade and Commerce (exports) and National Revenue (imports). International commitments are also met by cooperating with international inspectors from the International Atomic Energy Agency who carry out safeguards inspections under the international agreements to which Canada is a party.

Control over prescribed substances for purposes of safety is secured by the provision in the regulation that no person shall "produce, mine, prospect for, refine, use, sell or possess for any purpose prescribed substances except in accordance with a license issued by the AECB." The licensing process requires the prospective user to provide information on "the prescribed substance, its proposed application, operational safety, and physical security procedures and equipment; qualifications and experience of users, radio-active waste management plans and environmental consideration." If a license is issued the licensee is subject to the compliance inspections of the Board's inspection officers. Approximately 5,000 licenses are now in force with approximately 2,000 licenses (primarily radioisotopes) or amendments processed annually.[11]

The regulation of designated nuclear facilities and equipment (nuclear reactors for research and for power production, particle accelerators, mines, heavy water plants, large scale industrial and medical irradiators, uranium processing and fabrication plants, and radio-active waste management facilities) requires the prospective user or owner to secure a license to contruct and to operate such equipment.

The Atomic Energy Control Regulations set out the licensing procedures and requirements but also set out the maximum health and safety limits for the radioactivity released by the prescribed substances and facilities. The health and safety limits are largely derived from the recommendations of the International Commission of Radiological Protection (ICRP). The limits are based on a maximum radiation dose permitted to an individual. The AECB has established for all licensable activities a design and operating target of one percent of the maximum permissible exposures for the public whether acquired through gaseous effluents or liquid effluents.

By far the largest portion of the AECB's budget has been spent in fulfilling its statutory mandate to establish grants in aid for research in atomic energy. However, because of a growing feeling that these research grants have been oriented too much towards pure or basic oriented research as opposed to more applied research in support of its regulatory function, the AECB decided in 1976 to hand over this basic research granting role to the National Research Council and has since devoted its own R & D funding to work more directly needed in its regulatory role.

(c) Cabinet and Ministerial Policies

In addition to the above, nuclear decisions are shaped by and reflected in ministerial and cabinet policies, including those on energy generally, supply, safeguards, health and safety, licensing procedures, uranium foreign ownership, heavy water, and waste management.

(i) Energy and Foreign Policy

At their broadest level nuclear decisions are reflected in energy and foreign policy committments. The 1976 energy policy statement clearly envisaged that nuclear energy would assume a larger role among Canada's energy sources.[12] Prime Minister Trudeau directly linked nuclear and uranium to Canada's obligations to both western allies and the developing world. Statements accompanying the proposed 1977 <u>Nuclear Control and Administration Act</u> endorsed both the promotional economic benefits to Canada as well as the need for regulatory control. The position of the Clark Government has not been made clear though is not likely to be substantially different.

(ii) Uranium Supply Policy

The Honourable Donald S. Macdonald's September 1974 Statement on Uranium Policy[13] outlined measures to insure protection for Canadian uranium consumers in the face of heavy demands from other countries for long-term supplies of Canadian uranium. The policy was intended to insure two-fold protection:

o always to ensure long-term reserve of nuclear fuel for existing and committed reactors as well for reactors which are planned for operation in Canada for a ten-year period into the future;

o to ensure that sufficient uranium production capacity is available for the Canadian domestic nuclear power program to reach its full potential.

As a result of this policy statement (as opposed to a statutory instruction) the AECB is now required to ensure that a utility demonstrates that it is maintaining a contracted forward supply of nuclear fuel to enable each operating reactor to be operated at an annual capacity factor of 80 percent for at least 15 years, or for reactors committed but not yet operating for 15 years from their in-service dates. In addition, the AECB and other regulators of exports must now include, in their review of export licenses, consideration as to the adequacy of the exporting company's uncommitted uranium reserves to meet its share of the Canadian domestic reserve margin.

(iii) Safeguards Policy

A Safeguard Policy announced in the Honourable Donald S. Macdonald's Statement of December 20, 1974, is also of critical importance. The policy elaborated on and reinforced earlier Canadian foreign policy undertakings to ensure the peaceful uses of nuclear energy.[14] These undertakings had been enunciated earlier, including the Canadian commitment to the Non-Proliferation Treaty (NPLT). The December 20, 1974, statement was necessary because of the Government of India's nuclear explosion, an explosion using Canadian nuclear technology but developed in apparent contravention of the "peaceful purposes" undertaken in the Canada-India agreement. This event, when combined with the growing international demand for, and acceptance of CANDU, resulted in growing concern about the adequacy of nuclear safeguards. As pointed out in Chapters 2 and 3, the initial 1974 policy was strengthened in 1976 to include an insistence on full-scope safeguards for countries using or purchasing Canadian nuclear materials and equipment.

(iv) Uranium Mining and the Federal-Provincial Accommodation

Shortly after the passage of the Atomic Energy Control Act in 1946, representatives of the Province of Saskatchewan visited the AECB to point out that Saskatchewan had detailed regulations governing mining operations, and confusion would result if the Board were to attempt to set out special rules for prospecting, staking, development, and mining of uranium deposits. The Board agreed that provincial rules regarding prospecting and staking should apply, but a Board license[15] would be required during the development and mining stages.

In the early 1950's, private operators in Ontario were anxious to develop and mine previously known uranium deposits in that province. The AECB held discussions with officials of the Ontario Department of Mines concerning licensing arrangements. At this time, the Board's interests were directed to the security of the uranium and information regarding its reserves, production and disposition, and it was understood that the provincial authorities would take responsibility for the safety of the mines and the health of its workers. It was also agreed that the

Board in its exploration and mining licenses would impose a condition requiring compliance with provincial laws respecting mine safety. The actual wording agreed upon was as follows:

> That, subject to the Atomic Energy Control Regulations, any applicable provincial statutes and regulations, or the regulations affecting mining in the Northwest Territories and the Yukon, as the case may be, in so far as they deal with mine safety and cognate matters, are to be observed and complied with in relation to the said property and to all operations undertaken in connection therewith.[16]

The above wording has been included as a condition of all licenses issued by the Board to mine uranium to this date.

During the 1960's, there were repeated requests from provincial ministers of mines for the federal government to transfer jurisdiction over uranium mines to the provinces. At the Conference of the Provincial Ministers of Mines in September 1968, the Honourable J.J. Greene, then Minister of Energy, Mines and Resources, reiterated that, except in matters related to national security and foreign policy, uranium mines should be subject to the same rules as those which the provinces exercise over the mines.[17] He also expressed the wish and intention of the federal government that the provinces continue to be able to apply such controls. More explicitly, he indicated that although the Atomic Energy Control Act established federal government jurisdiction in matters relating to national security and foreign policy, in no way should it hinder or limit provisions to ensure the application of the rules applicable to other mines under provincial jurisdiction. He also referred to the AECB mining permits being conditional upon the licensee obtaining from the province concerned the necessary property rights, and, subject to the Atomic Energy Control Regulations, compliance with all applicable provincial and territorial regulations. He further stated that, wherever possible, the AECB would appoint provincial officials as inspectors under the health and safety sections of its regulations. These guidelines, which are still in operation, presupposed the existence of adequate regulatory provisions by the province and systems for maintaining them.

(v) <u>Licensing Policies and Procedures</u>

Applications for nuclear facility licences are normally made in three stages: site approval, construction approval and operating license. Site approval is further sub-divided into conditional site approval and final site approval. Conditional site approval may be given on the submission and acceptance of preliminary site evaluation reports and is normally transmitted by letter which indicates that AECB sees no major reason, on the basis of the information submitted, why final site approval may not be given. Before a final site approval is given, the applicant must have conducted a public information program (including public meetings to outline proposed plans and resultant environmental, social and economic impacts and to collect feedback from the interested public), satisfied environmental assessment and related requirements and submitted the final site evaluation report to the Board. Construction approval may be granted on submission of an application and the preliminary safety report, which includes design information and postulated accident analyses. The preliminary safety report is further developed and updated through the construction period and forms the basis for the operating licence submission. The operating license may be granted on application and submission of complete documentation including final safety report, operating policies and procedures, radiation protection manuals, etc., and assurances that design, construction and commissioning have been completed in accordance with all regulatory requirements. The operating licence is normally first issued as a provisional licence with subsequent approvals given to proceed with the various phases of commissioning. On satisfactory completion of commissioning, submission of outstanding documentation, and finalization of commissioning and operating assurances, the final operating licence may be issued.

In the case of nuclear facilities such as radioactive waste management sites, the AECB specifies that the decision to establish such facilities carries with it the obligation of owners for long-term surveillance of the site, both inside and outside, and of the environs some distance from the site. The length of time for whch surveillance may be required, upon abandonment of the site, will be determined by the specific radionuclides buried at the site.

Licences are normally issued for a fixed term and are renewable on application and on demonstration of satisfactory compliance with their terms and conditions. Licences may be cancelled or revoked at any time because of non-compliance, or in order to amend them.

Any shipment of prescribed substances must comply with packaging and labelling requirements and any other regulations established by an agency that has statutory authority in respect of the proposed method of transportation. In the absence of such authority, the regulations of the Canadian Transport Commission or the requirements established by the Atomic Energy Control Board apply. The AECB conducted a comprehensive study of incidents that occurred in the transportation of nuclear materials for the years 1957 to 1975. Out of a total of 402,210 shipments, only sixty-one incidents were reported; none of which resulted in serious damage or injuries.[18]

(vi)   Foreign Ownership of the Uranium Industry

In 1970, a policy on foreign ownership of the Canadian uranium industry was enunciated by Prime Minister Trudeau. An initiative of senior PCO officials which was seized by ministers, the policy arose when it was learned that Hudson Bay Oil and Gas, a foreign-owned company, was attempting to buy a controlling interest in Denision Mines Limited, controlled by Stephen Roman. On March 2, 1970, Prime Minister Trudeau expressed the government's disapproval of the impending sale and said that if necessary the government would act, through an amendment to the <u>Atomic Energy Control Act</u> to take effect on that date, to prevent such a transaction. Later in March, May and September of 1970 the Minister of Energy, Mines and Resources, the Honourable J.J. Greene, issued further statements. These gave notice that legislation would be passed to limit foreign ownership at the mining stage of any uranium property to 33 percent. Foreign owners of uranium companies were permitted to retain their holdings as of March 2, 1979, but any future sales of such holdings were to be made to Canadian residents until the total foreign ownership was reduced to 33 percent.[19] While the foreign ownership decision will not be examined it is worth noting as an aside that it is an excellent example of government intervention by means of raw power. The promised legislation was not passed nor has it been passed at time of writing (though provisions for its passage exist in the <u>Uranium and Thorium Mining Review Act</u> introduced in 1977 and then withdrawn), and uranium ownership has been monitored by the Foreign Investment Review Agency since 1975 under the <u>Foreign Investment Review Act</u>.

(vii) <u>Heavy Water</u>

As pointed out in Chapter 2, the production of heavy water has experienced periods of under-supply and recently over-supply. Federal policy has evolved from an initial preference in the 1960s to supply heavy water through contracts with the private sector, a policy which floundered after the failure of the Glace Bay and Port Hawkesbury plants.[20] This was followed by arrangements and agreements with Ontario Hydro in the late 1960s and early 1970s under which AECL supplied and pooled heavy water primarily through the Bruce Heavy Water Plant A. In 1972 as Ontario Hydro contemplated a major expansion of its nuclear program based on the success of its Pickering reactors, a federal-provincial dispute arose over priority of access to the pooled heavy water supply by non-Ontario reactors on the one hand, and the new Ontario demand on the other. By 1973, Ontario Hydro had assumed that it would have to take responsibility to ensure its own supply. It sought without success to obtain federal funding of new heavy plants and, in July 1973, purchased Bruce Heavy Water Plant A from

AECB. By 1973 federal policy had effectively become one of financing a province's initial step into a nuclear program but not thereafter. At the same time, the federal government announced it would build a new heavy water plant, La Prade, at Trois-Rivières, Quebec (to meet the needs of other utilities and of the export market). Later, after an "off again on again" construction history and the scaling down of nuclear construction plans, La Prade became the victim of federal expenditure cuts in August 1978 and was "mothballed".

The heavy water story is examined elsewhere[21], but policies regarding heavy water are of interest to us not only because they are an important part of the background of nuclear policy but also because they have become a source of federal-provincial conflict and hence effect the kinds of intervention that may occur in other aspects of nuclear policy, a fact to be illustrated more clearly in Chapter 8.

(viii) Waste Management

As we have stressed the long term management of radioactive wastes has been and is the source of immense controversy. In response to public criticism including demands that there be a moratorium of all further nuclear development until the waste management issue is resolved, the federal Department of Energy, Mines and Resources and the Ontario Ministry of Energy announced on June 8, 1978, a joint program on the first phase of a long term program to assure safe and permanent disposal of radio-active waste from nuclear power reactors.[22]

Prime responsibility for the program rests with the federal government. Its agencies will undertake R & D work on the immobilization and disposal of radio-active wastes. The Government of Ontario will be responsible for studies on interim storage and the transportation of irradiated fuel. The policy announcement made it clear that a Canadian position on the question of reprocessing of irradiated fuel was not to be established, pending the completion of the INFCE study.

(ix) Other Federal Environmental Controls

Nuclear facilities are also subject to the requirements of other federal environmental legislation administered by the federal Department of Fisheries and Environment. To use Saskatchewan as an example, the primary federal-provincial agreement affecting the Cluff Lake uranium development is the Canada-Saskatchewan Accord for the Protection and Enhancement of Environmental Quality.[23] The Accord is intended to ensure comprehensive programs to protect the environment, while avoiding duplication among agencies. Generally, the federal government agrees to establish national baseline effluent and emission standards for specific industrial groups and specific polutants, and the province agrees to establish and enforce requirements at least as stringent. Both parties also agree to cooperate in monitoring programs and to free exchange of data. While future control of uranium might be affected by this accord, the most direct federal "environmental" regulation arises out of the Metal Mining Liquid Effluent Regulations and Guidelines under the Fisheries Act.[24] These regulations apply to such projects as the Cluff Lake mine since it is a new mine. They prescribe arsenic, copper, lead, nickel, zinc total suspended matter and radium 226 as deleterious substances and set limits on these substances that may be discharged in effluents from the operations area of a mine-mill complex. The regulations further specify procedures and reporting requirements and prescribe acceptable disposal areas confined by proper natural or man-made structures. The guidelines accompanying the regulations are not legally binding but reflect what the department feels represents compliance with the spirit of the Fisheries Act. The regulations and guidelines were developed in close consultation with the AECB, other relevant federal agencies and provincial regulatory authorities including the Saskatchewan Department of Mineral Resources.

At the end of 1979, these controls have only recently been promulgated but it is expected, following practice in other areas, that the minimum national standards will be incorporated into licenses given to uranium mining companies by the Saskatchewan Departments of Minerals Resources, and Environment and by the AECB.

In the case studies which follow (Chapters 6, 7 and 8) we will have opportunity to see the impact of provincial policies and practices, particularly those of Ontario in which the nuclear power and uranium industry has been most concentrated. Accordingly, we will see at closer quarters the operation of various Ontario policies and agencies including Ontario Hydro and various mines, health, resource, labour and energy ministries. In earlier chapters we have already pointed out the different basis of Quebec and New Brunswick involvement. Quebec has been a reluctant nuclear partner and has preferred to link its energy development to James Bay and other hydro electric sources of power.[25] In the late 1970s Quebec policy is also profoundly influenced by the larger aspirations of the separatist Levesque government. New Brunswick was a more willing partner of the federal government although at time of writing even it has felt it necessary to hedge its bets by agreeing in principle to sell its lone nuclear reactor station at Lepreau to a new federal-provincial maritime energy corporation. Other provinces have only flirted with the possibility of nuclear power. Manitoba Hydro, until the election of the NDP government in 1969, seemed bent on a limited nuclear future, but has since withdrawn. British Columbia has begun to contemplate a nuclear future but with great caution and with its initial interest spurred by promising uranium finds. In the 1979 Prince Edward Island election the newly elected Conservative Government committed itself to a non-nuclear future. The Saskatchewan involvement has been limited to uranium rather than nuclear power. The discovery in the 1970s of enormous uranium resources in that province has required the province to strengthen its nuclear policy capability.[26]

The initial basis for provincial control and regulation arises out of its control of the ownership of resources (including hydro electric power and uranium) and of the need to determine proprietary rights to those firms interested in such resource development.

The province has also been involved in respect of some its power over labour relations and health although the constitutional basis of this activity in uranium development has never been directly tested.

NOTES: Chapter 5

1. The analysis of policy organization and process is based primarily on numerous interviews conducted by the author with knowledgeable officials at the federal and provincial levels of government.

2. See Gordon Sims, "The Evolution of AECL", unpublished M.A. thesis, Carleton University, Ottawa, 1979, and G. Bruce Doern, Nuclear Policy and State Enterprise (manuscript in preparation for Institute of Public Administration of Canada).

3. G. Bruce Doern and Peter Aucoin (eds.) Public Policy in Canada: Organization, Process and Management (Toronto: Macmillan of Canada, 1979) Chapter 2; and C. Campbell and G. Szablowski, The Superbureaucrats (Toronto: Macmillan of Canada, 1979).

4. See Ranger Uranium Environmental Inquiry, First Report (Canberra: Australian Government Publishing Service, 1976); Royal Commission on Environmental Pollution, Sixth Report, Nuclear Power and the Environment (London: H.M.S.O., 1976); and Ian Breach, Windscale Fallout (London: Penguin Books, 1978).

5. Unpublished polls taken by AECL confirmed the marked growth in opposition after these events. See M. Barrados, "The Impact of the Harrisburgh Accident on Canadian Public Opinion of Nuclear Power" (Ottawa: AECL, July 1979).

6. Royal Commission on Electric Power Planning, A Race Against Time (Toronto: Ontario Queen's Printer, 1978), Chapters 2 and 3.

7. Department of Energy, Mines and Resources, A Brief Submitted to the Cluff Lake Board of Inquiry, Regina, Saskatchewan, April 1977, pp. 6-7.

8. Atomic Energy Control Board, Brief to Cluff Lake Board of Inquiry, Regina, Saskatchewan, April 1977.

9. See "Highlights of Bill C-14 the proposed new Nuclear Control Act," Nuclear Canada Year Book (Toronto: Canadian Nuclear Association, April 1978).

10. See Canada Gazette, Part II, Vol. 108, No. 12, June 26, 1974. Later amendments are in Canada Gazette, Part II, Vol. 112, No. 2, June 25, 1978, and Vol. 113, No. 11, June 13, 1979.

11. G. Bruce Doern, The Atomic Energy Control Board, (Ottawa: Law Reform Commission of Canada, 1977).

12. Department of Energy, Mines and Resources, An Energy Policy for Canada (Ottawa: Minister of Supply and Services, 1976).

13. Statement by the Honourable Donald S. Macdonald, Minister of Energy, Mines and Resources on Canada's Uranium Policy, September 5, 1974.

14. See R.W. Morrison and E. Wonder, "Nuclear Export Policy," in G. Doern and R.W. Morrison (eds.) Canadian Nuclear Policies (Montreal: Institute for Research on Public Policy, 1980), Chapter 4.

15. Atomic Energy Control Board, Brief to the Royal Commission on the Health and Safety of Workers in Mines in Ontario. June 3, 1975.

16. Ibid., p. 8.

17. Ibid., p. 9.

18. Atomic Energy Control Board, A Brief Submitted to Cluff Lake Board of Enquiry, Regina, Saskatchewan, April 1977, p. 11.

19. Energy, Mines and Resources, <u>Brief Submitted to Cluff Lake Board of Enquiry</u>, Regina, Saskatchewan, April 1977, p. 51.

20. See G. Sims, <u>op. cit.</u>, chapter 7.

21. <u>Ibid</u>.

22. Malcolm Rowan, "Nuclear Policy and Federal Provincial Relations", in Doern and Morrison (eds.) <u>op. cit.</u>, Chapter 14. More generally, see F.K. Hare et al. <u>The Management of Canada's Nuclear Wastes</u> (Ottawa: Department of Energy, Mines and Resources, 1977).

23. Cluff Lake Board of Inquiry, <u>Hearings</u>, p. 965.

25. L. Amyot, "Nuclear Power in Quebec," in Doern and Morrison (eds.) <u>op. cit.</u>, Chapter 15.

26. Cluff Lake Board of Inquiry, <u>Final Report</u> (Regina: Saskatchewan Queen's Printer, 1978).

PART B: THREE CASE STUDIES IN GOVERNMENT INTERVENTION

Chapter 6

Intervention and Industrial Development: The CANDU Reactor Program*

The development of the unique CANDU power reactor program in the 1950s under the cooperative auspices of two government-owned corporations, AECL and Ontario Hydro, is one of the few examples in Canadian history where an industry from the outset was launched and nurtured through the vehicle of state enterprise. Other crown corporations have of course been created but usually after an industry has been developed and some form of greater governmental presence is deemed desirable. We have already characterized the nuclear industry in previous chapters as being a state industry. Though its birth in the heavy security environment of the Second World War made state control inevitable, it was not necessarily inevitable that the later reactor power program would be as extensively in the hands of government-owned corporations as it has become. Indeed this chapter will show that at one stage a far larger private sector component was envisaged.

This case study focuses on the use of state enterprise as a vehicle of intervention to achieve high technology based industrial development. The chapter

---

* This chapter is the product of a joint endeavour by myself and Gordon Sims. In addition to the published sources it is based on numerous interviews we conducted with knowledgeable current and retired AECL, Ontario Hydro and industry officials.

is organized into six sections. The first section will outline the main technical controversies which emerged in the 1950s. These will be related in the second section to the concurrent developments in the reactor programs of other countries. In section three the specific stages and issues in the development of the early CANDU program will be described with the focus on the first two power reactors, the Nuclear Power Demonstration reactor and the Douglas Point reactor. The Douglas Point decision will then be analyzed in section four in the context of both the technological determinants of government intervention and the reversal of the earlier enunciated policy of heavy private sector involvement. Finally, we offer some observations about the issues of intervention revealed by the case study.

(1) Technical Issues in the 1950s

The prospect of using nuclear energy as a source of power had been apparent since the first discovery of the fission process. In fact, the Paris atomic research group had applied for patents for this application before the German invasion of France caused them to flee to England.[1] But in the early 1950s the production of nuclear power that would be commercially competitive with existing power sources promised to be very difficult. A nuclear reactor capable of producing high temperature steam to drive electrical generators would have to compete with other methods of steam production such as burning coal or oil.

By the time AECL was created in 1952, several countries had research reactors and some of these had thermal heat outputs of several megawatts. The heat from these reactors was at a low temperature which made it unsuitable for electricity generation. It was simply being dumped either by air cooling into the atmosphere or by cooling water into the nearest body of water. In order to drive an electrical generator successfully the heat would have to be turned into steam at a temperature of several hundreds of degrees fahrenheit.[2] A brief description of some of the difficulties of this process will illustrate the problems facing the early designers of power reactors.

Some form of fluid is necessary to cool a reactor and transfer its heat to an electrical generating system. The cheapest and most readily available coolants are water and air. If water is used the entire nuclear heating system had to be pressurized so that the water can be converted to high temperature steam. If air were used as coolant this difficulty would not arise since the air could be heated to several hundred degrees fahrenheit and then used to produce high temperature steam in a pressurized water system reactor. Unfortunately, ordinary air could not be used for cooling at elevated temperatures since it would be highly oxidizing and therefore corrosive. Carbon dioxide could be a less corrosive, plentiful and cheap substitute.

Both water and carbon dioxide were used as coolants in some early reactors, and water has continued to be used in pressurized water and boiling light water reactors. Other coolant materials such as helium gas, high boiling-point organic liquids and liquid sodium were also considered. The first is rare and therefore expensive to use, but the last two are cheaper and more plentiful and both were used in some early reactor experiments. Sodium as a coolant was a particular interest as a heat transfer medium in very high temperature breeder reactors. Although low temperature reactors had been built in the U.S.A. during the war for plutonium production, it was realised that much more efficient production of plutonium could be achieved with high temperture (i.e., fast) neutrons. A high temperature reactor promised to "breed" more fissionable plutonium than was consumed in the form of uranium, since during its operation it would produce plutonium from the non-fissionable uranium-238. The quanity of uranium available in the world was expected to be limited and a breeder system which could extend the amount of power available from uranium was clearly desirable, particularly for countries such as the U.K. and France which did not possess adequate domestic uranium resources.

Another major problem facing reactor designers was the choice of material to be used to moderate the neutrons, to slow them down so that they could be efficiently captured by uranium-235 nuclei to keep the chain reaction going. It was necessary that the material used have a very low capacity to absorb neutrons, so that the chain reaction could be kept going with a minimum loss of neutrons to the moderator. As was seen earlier, light water (ordinary water) had been used, but its absorption capacity for neutrons was too high to allow a self-sustaining chain reaction with natural uranium. However, it would be possible to use it if the uranium were partially enriched in the fissionable isotope uranium-235. If enriched uranium were not available, two other materials could be used as moderators with natural uranium: carbon and heavy water. The former was cheap and plentiful but had higher neutron absorption properties than the latter. Heavy water promised the best neutron economy but it was difficult to produce and therefore expensive.

A third major problem confronting reactor designers was the choice of materials to be used inside the reactor core as structural materials for containing the moderator and cooling fluids, and for encasing the uranium. Aluminum had low neutron absorption properties but was lacking in structural strength and had a strong tendency to corrade at high temperatures. Zirconium had better nuclear, corrosion and structural possibilities but this was a fairly rare material at that time and not too much was known about this metal and its alloys.

Some of the problems mentioned above could possibly be circumvented by dissolving partially enriched uranium in water and using this solution as the reactor core. This type of homogeneous reactor was used experimentally, but the concept was not as efficient as some of the other alternatives and it was eventually discarded.

During the years after the war several countries were examining the possibility of producing power from fission and were considering the many approaches that were possible. In Canada in 1951, W.B. Lewis at Chalk River has prepared "An Atomic Power Prosposal"[3] for a power reactor to be produced in Canada. The proposal called for a natural uranium fuelled, heavy water mederated and cooled reactor, pressurized to 1,500 lbs./square inch with a steam outlet temperature of 550 degrees fahrenheit. The proposal also contained the suggestion that if aluminum proved to be unsuitable at these high operating temperatures and pressures, zirconium could be used as an alternative. Lewis realized that since there were so many unkown factors in the production of nuclear power, his economic assessment of its cost was a highly speculative endeavour. It was clear that at the time AECL was formed, the possibility of nuclear power generation was being considered at Chalk River, but no committment had been made and would not be made for more than a year.

Before considering Canada's development of nuclear power, the programs being considered and/or underway in other countries will be examined briefly in order to place Canada's effort in a world context. In this way the unique character of the Canadian effort will be high-lighted, particularly the high risk nature of Canada's decision to follow its own technological course.

(2) Overseas Power Reactor Programs

(a) The United States

The American power reactor program started on January 1, 1947 when the United States Atomic Energy Commission (USAEC) inherited the ground-work in low temperature reactor technology from its military predecessor, the Army Corps of Engineers.[4]

As part of its management of the Manhattan Project, the Army had built several plutonium production reactors and several small experimental reactors. After considering the possibilities for action, the USAEC started to move as its predecessor had done, on a broad front, trying to cover simultaneously as many options as possible. Construction of a high neutron flux materials test reactor was authorized since much more had to be known of the long term effects of neutron bombardment on the materials being used to construct reactors. An experimental fast breeder reactor was started, designed to produce more nuclear fuel than it consumed. A third project, which was to prove most significant in the future of the U.S. power program, was the development of a compact prototype pressurized water reactor for submarine propulsion. The technology developed for this prototype was later to be applied to produce the large pressurized water reactor which became one of the most successful reactors in the American nuclear power program.[5] As the work progressed the program was broadened to include the construction of an experimental homogeneous reactor, a sodium cooled, graphite moderated reactor, and an experimental boiling water reactor. This broad approach of developing several reactor types simultaneously could only be adopted in a country with an industrial and economic base as large as the United States.

By 1954 it was apparent that the U.S. prime emphasis would be on the development of two types of light water reactors (LWRs), the pressurized light water (PWR) and the boiling light water reactors (BWR).[6] The former was represented by the 60 megawatt reactor at Shippingport built by Westinghouse which went critical in 1957,[7] and the latter by the 180 megawatt Dresden 1 reactor built by General Electric (GE) which went into service in 1959. It should be noted that the first Canadian reactor, the 20 megawatt NPD, did not go critical until 1962.

In 1955 the USAEC encouraged the participation of electrical utilities in the nuclear power program by an offer to finance the reactor portion of a nuclear station. However, by late 1962 only one full-scale (575 megawatt) station had been committed, the Connecticut Yankee PWR being built by Westinghouse.

In 1963 a major breakthough was announced with the order of a 515 megawatt BWR from GE to be build at Osyter Creek. This plant was projected to be expanded to 640 megawatts and at this latter output the plant would cost $108 per kilowatt, a price competitive with current fossil fuel stations.[8] Interest by the U.S. utilities began to mount rapidly. Six LWRs were ordered in 1965, three from Westinghouse and three from GE. Eighteen units were ordered in 1966 and 30 units with an average capacity of over 850 megawatts were ordered in 1967. Clearly, by the late 1970s nuclear energy had been "... accepted, even embraced, by the US nuclear and electrical utility industries."[9] For comparison, it should be noted that the first Canadian commerical nuclear power station at Pickering was committed in 1964, but subsequent developments, being confined mainly to the province of Ontario, did not enjoy the spectacular expansion of the American program.

Of the other experimental reactor types which the U.S. investigated, substantial work toward commercialization had only been carried out on the fast breeder. Progress has been slow and the first 350 megawatt station, which was expected to be in service in 1983,[10] has recently been the subject of sharp controversy within the American government which has placed its continuation in doubt.

(b) <u>The United Kingdom</u>

The U.K. nuclear program did not get underway until well after the end of the war. At first it was dominated by the decision made in January 1947 that Britain should posess its own atomic bomb.[11] This decision was made in the interests of national independence following the withdrawal of nuclear collaboration by the United States after the end of the war. This culminated in the passage of the <u>McMahon Act</u> in August 1946, which prohibited the transmission of restricted atomic data by the USA to any other country. It arose from fears of security leaks to Russia and these fears had been heightened by the disclosure in February 1946 that Alan Nunn-May, a member of the Montreal team in Canada, had been passing atomic information to the Russians.

The first step in the British program involved the construction of two low temperature, air-cooled, graphite moderated reactors at Windscale to produce plutonium. With this experience behind them, it was natural that when a decision to construct a power reactor was made early in 1953, a similar type of reactor should be chosen. Since then power reactor was to operate at a much higher temperature than the production reactor, carbon dioxide was used as a heat transfer medium instead of air. Pressurized or boiling water reactors could not have been considered since they required enriched uranium. Although enrichment facilities were being built at Capenhurst in the U.K., it was not expected that they would be completed before 1956. Even then only small quantities of enriched uranium would be available at first. If natural uranium were to be used as fuel, graphite was the only moderator which could be considered since heavy water was not available in the U.K. Also Britain had informally foresworn an interest in heavy water power reactors, regarding this as Canada's province.[12] Other factors in the decision were that the graphite moderated, gas-cooled reactor promised to be the cheapest reactor to construct,[13] and was also one of the safest reactor types. This latter consideration was of importance in a small, densely-populated country where any reactor would necessarily be close to large population centres.[14] In addition, it was thought at the time that these reactors would only be an interim stage in power reactor development before a fast breeder reactor took over. A design study of an experimental fast breeder, to be eventually located at Dounreay in Scotland, was started in 1951.[15]

The first power reactor, which was built at Calder Hall, was a dual purpose type for the production of power and plutonium. Its output was 35 megawatts and the cost of electricity produced by it was only competitive with other sources of power if allowance was made for the value of the plutonium which was also produced. It was to go into operation in 1956 as the first of a series of reactors of this general type which were to be produced in the U.K.

Although nine stations modeled on Calder Hall have been operating reliably with high load factors, they have poor neutron economy and do not make efficient use of their uranium. They have been likened to the horizontal beam engine of the nuclear age; sturdy and reliable but obsolete.[16]

In 1964 the U.K. Atomic Energy Authority decided to select a new reactor type. The choice was between the BWR system developed by GE in the U.S., and a domestically designed Advanced Gas Reactor (AGR).[17] A decision was made in favour of the AGR but the program was soon in trouble. Technical problems began to occur in attempts to scale up to 660 megawatts, and the first two units have not yet been completed although other units which were started later have already been comissioned.[18]

By 1972 it was clear that the AGR would not be economical to operate and after considerable delay and controversy, a further choice was made among a British designed steam generating heavy water reactor (SGHWR), the Canadian CANDU, a high temperature gas reactor and the American PWR. The SGHWR was selected in 1974 but again it appears that the wrong choice has been made. the SGHWR program has not been successful and the British are now favouring the PWR.

Meanwhile, the 60 megawatt Dounreay fast breeder reactor had gone critical in 1959 and subsequently a 250 megawatt prototype was built and commissioned in 1976. But, as in the United States, the fast breeder program in the U.K. is progressing much more slowly than was originally anticipated.

(c) France

In France, as in the U.S. and Britain, the initial impulse for the development of nuclear reactors came from a desire to obtain plutonium for military purposes. In France, as in the U.K., a start was made with the simplest type of reactor designed to get into the nuclear business as soon as possible. This meant constructing graphite moderated, gas-cooled reactors which were designed to produce both electricity and plutonium.[19]

The first reactor was a graphite moderated, air-cooled reactor to be used solely for plutonium production (c.f. the U.K. Windscale reactors).[20] The second was a graphite moderated, carbon dioxide cooled reactor for both power and plutonium production (c.f. the UK Calder Hall reactors) designed to be in operation in 1957.[21]

France also mounted a program to develop a breeder reactor because, like the U.K., France had no secure access to uranium supplies and a breeder system promised a large degree of independence in this respect. The French breeder program has had considerable success with the 240 megawatt Marcould Phenix going into service in 1974 and the 1,200 megawatt Super Phenix scheduled for operation in 1980.

Following the construction of its prototype power reactors, the major French effort continued with the gas cooled, graphite moderated system and Electricité de France (EdF) planned a series of three of these reactors at Chinon in the Loire valley with power ratings of 70, 240 and 500 megawatts. These stations went critical in 1962, 1965 and 1967 respectively.[22]

However EdF and the French nuclear consortia viewed themselves as becoming technologically isolated and unable to compete for overseas sales with this type of reactor and pressured the government to allow them to build LWRs as their next generation series of reactors. For a while the French aversion to relying on American technology held firm, but by the end of 1968 the government announced a decision to go ahead with the construction of a 600 megawatt light water reactor. Contracts were subsequently awarded for both PWRs and BWRs but financial constraints led to the cancellation of the latter.[23]

Framatome emerged as the major consortium since it held a Westinghouse PWR license, and French industry has adapted to the new technology so well that Framatome is now a major nuclear exporter.[24]

(d) The Soviet Union

Little was known of the Russian developments in nuclear power until the first Geneva Conference on the

Peaceful Uses of Atomic Energy in 1955. At that conference the Russians presented a paper describing their first nuclear station which produced power on 27 June 1954.[25] It was a water cooled graphite moderated reactor using five percent enriched uranium as fuel and producing about five megawatts of electrical power.[26]

The Russian reactor program at first followed a pattern similar to the American program with a variety of research reactor types being built to gain experience. Some of these were pursued to the prototype power reactor stage, such as the light water graphite reactor (LWGR) mentioned above, a BWR, a boiling light water graphite reactor (BEGR) and a PWR.[27] In the mid-1960s Soviet planners chose to standarize on the BWGR and the PWR. Both types experienced their share of technological and cost difficulties, but a commercial-sized BWGR rated at 200 megawatts went into operation in 1967, and a 354 megawatts PWR went critical in late 1969.

Since then the Russians have moved to rapidly expand their nuclear program and pairs of BWGRs with outputs greater than 1,000 megawatts are planned for sites near Leningrad, Smolensk, Kiev, and Bursk.[28] Even though this suggests the BWGR is preferred to the PWR, all of the Russian reactors exported to Eastern Europe have been of the PWR design.[29]

(3) The Canadian Nuclear Power Program

When Canada committed itself to build a 20 megawatt prototype reactor at the end of 1954, the United States had already started its 60 megawatt pressurized water reactor in 1953 and was about to embark on its ambitious and diverse Power Reactor Demonstration Program to develop several types of reactors simultaneously. The U.K. had begun a 35 megawatt reactor at Calder Hall in 1953 with a projected completion date of 1956, and France was following with a similar reactor system about one year behind the U.K. Even Russia had produced its first nuclear power by 1954.

The Canadian program centred from the beginning on the heavy water moderated and cooled reactor system. The Canadian decision to ignore progress in other countries and develop a unique system was a risky one. At the same time it must be admitted that two unique circumstances paved the way for the decision. The first was the experience with heavy water technology with the research reactor NRX. The second was the presence of large stocks of uranium in Canada which meant that this country, unlike the U.K. and France, did not have to think in terms of a cheap and quick interim reactor system to tide it over until breeder reactors could be developed. This latter point also meant that the Canadian effort had a single focus, which was also necessary in view of the limited effort that could be applied by a small country.

When AECL was created as a Crown corporation in 1952, one of the major reasons for separating it from the National Research Council (NRC) was the increasing commercial nature of its activities. These activities were associated with the research reactors at Chalk River since there was at that time no commitment by the Canadian government to engage in the commercial exploitation of nuclear power.

The NRX reactor was producing plutonium for the USAEC and the NRU reactor (U for universal) committed at the end of 1950, promised to increase revenues from this source considerably. AECL was also renting "loops" in the NRX reactor to the USAEC and between the revenues from plutonium sales and loop rentals was earning several million dollars per year.[30]

Despite the lack of commitment to nuclear power, the possibility of producing it was under active discussion during 1952. These discussions included not only Chalk River personnel, but also the president of AECL, Dr. C.J. MacKenzie, a member of the Board (R.L. Hearn who was also the chairman of the Hydro Electric Power Commission of Ontario, HEPCO), and the federal government represented by C.D. Howe, the Minister of Trade and Commerce.

The first indication that the government was actively considering a nuclear power program for Canada came in early 1953 when, during the course of a debate in the House of Commons, Howe stated:

> Here in Canada we believe that the time has come to undertake the development of atomic power in this country, and discussions are going on as to ways and means of bringing about that development. We feel that the production of power is the concern of those who distribute power, organizations like the Hydro Electric Power Commission of Ontario, or the major privately owned power companies.[31]

AECL was not only successful in pressing its views on the Government, it also took care to impress those M.P.s who, from time to time, visited the Chalk River establishment. Its success may be gauged by the following quotations taken from the Debates of the House of Commons:

> I must say that I was much impressed by the spirit of the young Canadians who are carrying on this atomic energy work of Canada. I have never encountered such high morale or esprit de corps as we found at Chalk River and Deep River except in the Canadian corps during the late years of the first war ... as one of them expressed it to me, "Oh, this is so exciting, I would not leave for anything."[32]

> Dr. MacKenzie and his splendid group of young scientists gave us every opportunity to see and learn ... were extremely courteous in every way.[33]

> I have been deeply impressed by the ability and by the energy of the scientific officers who are directing the work of those young scientists who are occupied in the actual development of the project itself.[34]

With the support of the government and the sometimes enthusiastic approval of parliamentarians, AECL began a power reactor feasibility study in early 1954. Its objective was "the determination of an outline specification for a small or prototype power reactor."[35]

(a) The Nuclear Power Demonstration Reactor (NPD)

The study team was headed by Harold Smith of HEPCO (Ontario Hydro) and included representatives from the power utilities (HEPCO, British Columbia Electric Co., Shawnigan Water and Power Co., and Manitoba Hydro) and industry (Canadian Brazilian Services, Montreal Engineering Co., and Babcock and Wilson Co.).[36] It was obvious that AECL would have to play a lead role in this study. But even at this early stage the future involvement of the company in reactor production was seen as being limited to providing advice on the nuclear aspects of reactor production without any involvement in design and construction.

> Under the arrangement contemplated, AECL will supply all the necessary nuclear data and will be responsible for performance from a nuclear stand-point. The contracting firm will be responsible for design and construction and for mechanical performance.[37]

AECL clearly envisioned that Canadian industry would not only have to provide the facilities and expertise for reactor construction, a role which it would be currently well-equipped to play, but that this expertise would also have to extend back a further stange to the actual design of nuclear reactors. In its role as primarily a research and development organization, AECL would provide a support role in providing nuclear data, but the application of this data to design and construction was beyond its conception of its responsibilities.[38] The formation of the study group to examine the feasibility of nuclear power production involved Canadian industry from the outset and descriptions of industrial involvement in nuclear power were a major section in most of the AECL Annual Reports of this period.[39]

This policy was successful during the construction of the first prototype reactor but it was subsequently abandoned with AECL accepting the major role in the design and construction activities. This policy change has been a major factor in the development of AECL and the reasons behind it are the focus of this case study in intervention.

The design study for a small prototype nuclear power reactor was successfully concluded in 1954 and in December of that year AECL invited proposals from industry and the utilities for the construction and operation respectively of the nuclear station. Seven industrial companies were solicited and all were advised that they would have to make some financial contribution towards the project.[40] As a result of the proposals received, AECL recommended and the Government agreed, that Canadian General Electric Ltd. (CGE) should be awarded the contract.

The major reason for selecting CGE was its offer to contribute $2 million to the design and construction of the reactor. This $2 million was not to be a cash transfer to the government but was to be contributed in design and manufacturing services. The fact that CGE was a major Canadian electrical manufacturer added credibility to its bid. The involvement of the parent U.S. company, General Electric Corp., in the American nuclear power program was also seen as a positive asset.[41]

Two utilities, the Hydro Electric Power Commission of Ontario (HEPCO, later to be known as Ontario Hydro) and the Nova Scotia Light and Power Company Ltd., made specific proposals for partipation in the project, and two other utilities indicated some interest. AECL recommended, and the Government approved, that the proposal of HEPCO be accepted. The reason for the choice of HEPCO was based on several factors. First, because of the large size of the electrical grid being operated by HEPCO, the introduction of an experimental station with its attendant possibilities of power failures and interruptions would cause a minimum disruption in its power supply. Second, a site could be chosen by HEPCO which would be convenient to Chalk River. Third, HEPCO had made a major contribution to the feasibility study on which the specifications for the demonstration reactor would be based. Fourth, the HEPCO proposal offered to share costs - and losses - on the project in the event of failure.[42]

HEPCO also had a major incentive to explore the nuclear option that did not apply to most of the other Canadian utilities. The sources of hydro electric power in Ontario were increasingly being fully utilized and further additions to the power network would have to be provided by fossil fuel stations. Situated between the coal fields in Western and Eastern Canada (i.e., Cape Breton) and with no reliable access to either, the Ontario utility would have to import its coal from the Pennsylvania fields in the U.S. Nuclear power, if it were economically viable, would provide a highly desirable indigenous souce of power for Ontario.[43] The early realization that nuclear power, if it ever were to be used economically, would have to be produced by a large power station also worked in favour of HEPCO, since as was later pointed out by Gordon Churchill, "The amount of electric power that will be produced by CANDU could be utilized by a grid system as large as the present one in Ontario."[44]

As early as 1960 AECL was reporting that Ontario had estimated a need for as much as 7,000 megawatts of nuclear power by 1980.[45] In fact, when the Pickering B station is completed in 1981-83, Ontario will have just over 7,000 megawatts of nuclear power in operation. This is probably one of the few accurate long range forecasts of nuclear power requirements ever made anywhere in the world!

The estimated cost of the prototype reactor, which was to be called NPD (Nuclear Power Demonstration), was $14.5 million. Of this sum AECL was to provide $9 million, HEPCO $3.5 million and CGE $2 million.[46] HEPCO was to provide the site and the conventional part of the station (turbines, generators, etc.), CGE was responsible for the design and construction of the nuclear part of the station and AECL was to provide data required for the design of the nuclear part and be responsible for performance from a nuclear standpoint. The estimated completion date was early 1958.[47]

With these multi-million dollar expenditures, first on NRU and now NPD, concern over the cost of Canada's nuclear program was beginning to appear even at this early stage. On March 1st, 1956, Mr. Howard C. Green stated in the House of Commons:

> At present large sums of money are being spent in this field [atomic energy] and there is an increase in the estimates for the current year. Yet parliament has practically no way of checking these particular expenditures.... There is almost a complete lack of information given to the House about what is happening in this particular field.[48]

The Government responded on August 5, 1956, by providing the estimated net cash requirements by AECL requested for the next five years. The figures below given to the House are compared with AECL expenditures for the five years as reported in the AECL Annual Reports:

Year	Estimated	Actual
1956-57	$36 million	$31 million
1957-58	$30 million	$25 million
1958-59	$20 million	$29 million
1959-60	$13 million	$31 million
1960-61	$15 million	$38 million

Part, but not all, of the increase in the actual expenditures over the estimates were due to cost overruns on NPD. Though AECL forcast a general decrease in expenditures as shown above, AECL annual expenditures have shown steady annual increases following the decrease recorded for 1957-58.

One reason for the cost overrun on NPD was that the design underwent considerable change about a year after the project started. The original design called for the nuclear reactor to be contained inside a pressure vessel. The manufacturing capability for large, high-pressure containment vessels did not exist in Canada and this item would have had to be imported. It would clearly be preferable to use a modular pressure-tube design, but the tubes would have to possess good mechanical and corrosion resistance properties together with a low capacity to absorb neutrons. Such a material did not exist when the design phase for NPD started. Shortly thereafter, however, the U.S. Bettis Laboratory at Pittsburgh succeeded in developing an alloy of zirconium, Zircaloy-2, which had the necessary properties and this made the pressure tube concept practicable.

This material had been tested in the NRX reactor at Chalk River since 1953 as part of the Canada-U.S. collaborative program so that the designers at AECL had the confidence in it to specify it for use in a reactor.[49] As a result, NPD was redesigned to use the pressure-tube concept in which bundles of uranium fuel were contained in individual tubes as part of the reactor core.[50]

This arrangement lead to another design change since now the changing of fuel could be done on an individual tube-by-tube basis while the reactor was still operating, with fresh fuel being inserted at one end of the pressure tube and spent fuel being extracted from the other. A special re-fuelling machine was designed which could be remotely controlled to index on to any one of the tubes for fuel insertion or extraction. NPD now contained all the basic features which were to make the CANDU series of reactors which were to follow it unique among the world's power reactor types. It was fuelled by natural uranium, moderated and cooled by heavy water, had a horizontal pressure tube core arrangement and could be re-fuelled while on power.

(b) The Douglas Point Reactor

The Nuclear Power Demonstration (NPD) was not expected to produce electricity on an economically competitive basis with other power stations being operated in Canada at that time. It was intended to prove the principle of a nuclear power reactor and also provide more realistic cost estimates which could be applied to a larger station. There were grounds for believing that a large reactor could be competitive with existing coal-fired power stations. To achieve this it would be necessary to construct a station with an output of one or more hundreds of megawatts, rather than the 20 megawatts which was the design output of NPD. When the feasibility study for NPD was completed in 1954, a decision was made by AECL to undertake a preliminary design study with associated development programs for a large power reactor capable of producing 100 megawatts of electricity.[51] This study was undertaken by the NPD design team and when it was completed in 1957 the power output of the proposed reactor had risen to 200 megawatts. The preliminary estimated cost was $60 million. In February, 1958, government approval was obtained to start a four year program of engineering development for the new reactor.[52]

A new division of AECL, Nuclear Power Plant Division, was set up in Toronto to direct engineering development on the large reactor and to coordinate the NPD program. However, industry and utility involvement in Canada's nuclear power program was to continue.

> All the Canadian utilities and those manufactures who are now engaged in the program or who have an interest in the program will be invited to contribute staff to the new division. In this way we hope to provide for the most effective participation of the utilities and the manufactures in the development of economic nuclear power.[53]

The estimated cost of the program for the next five years was $140 million, of which $100 million would be for research and development and $40 million for the completion of NPD and the completion of the engineering development phase of the 200 megawatt CANDU reactor. The mounting expenditures did not seem to worry the leaders of the opposition since both Mr. Pearson (Lib.) and Mr. Knowles (CCF) welcomed the government statement.[54]

The four-year development phase for the new reactor was only sixteen months old when, in June 1959, upon the recommendation of the Board of AECL, the government authorized the company to begin construction of the 200 megawatt reactor. This was done <u>without waiting</u> for the completion of its design and development phase, or the NPD station (begun in early 1955) to go into operation.

> This decision to proceed was based on the confidence in the design, the experience provided from the NPD design, the success of the fuel development program at Chalk River, and on the realization that a full-scale plant must be built and operated before real costs of large stations can be know.[55]

The new station was to be built by AECL at Douglas Point, Ontario, in collaboration with Ontario Hydro, with AECL paying for the costs of the station and Ontario Hydro providing the site and some staff and services. The completed station would be operated by Ontario Hydro as a unit in its power system at maximum practical capacity and Hydro would buy the power produced.[56] The rates would be the same as it would otherwise have to pay to obtain the equivalent power from other sources.

Ontario Hydro had also agreed to purchase the station. AECL stated:

> After the station has demonstrated its performance Ontario Hydro will purchase the station from AECL for a sum calculated

to represent the worth of the station to
Ontario Hydro taking into account its performance, the cost of fuel, the capital
charge rates, the cost of alternative
coal-fire energy sources and other similar
factors.[57]

The estimated cost of the station as provided to
the government by AECL was now $81.5 million. However, since the design and development phase had not
been completed, tenders for components had not been
called, so that accurate costs were not known.

It appears that under this arrangement the government of Canada had approved the manufacture of a
nuclear power reactor without knowing accurately the
cost of the station. Furthermore the cost of the
station, or some undefined portion of it which would
not be known for many years, would later be reimbursed
to the government by Ontario Hydro if the costs of
nuclear power exceeded those of conventional sources.

With regard to the cost of the reactor, the government's faith in AECL seems to have been justified
for the cost of constructing the station was $77.6
million (without interest charges), i.e., below the
$81.5 million originally estimated. But Ontario Hydro
has never exercised its agreement to purchase the reactor from AECL. The station was declared "in service" on September 26, 1969[58] but was still having
teething problems. Most of these had been cleared up
by 1971, but eight years later Hydro has still not
bought the station. At present, the station is producing revenue for AECL from the electricity and steam
it is selling to Hydro and on April 1, 1977, the company determined that the station is principally a
commercial activity and the operating results would be
included in the future as part of the Commercial Operations.[59] The accrued interest on the loan used to
build the station was discharged by obtaining a Parliamentary appropriation on March 31, 1977.[60] The
Douglas Point station is now being carried as a depreciating item on the books of the company. Any hope
that Ontario Hydro will eventually purchase it appears
to have disappeared.

(4) The Douglas Point Decision - Technological
     Leapfrogging

The speed with which the nuclear program was being pushed may appear surprising. The decision to start the preliminary design work on the larger reactor before the prototype was completed; the further decision to proceed with the large reactor before the design and development work on it was completed and before any operating experience had been gained with the prototype, all seem to show evidence of undue haste. But it should be remembered that this was a time when technological triumphs were an accepted fact of life whether they were as awesome as a fusion bomb or as thrilling as a Sputnik.

An atmosphere of competitiveness between the three major nuclear power establishments was also a motivating factor for the management of AECL. In mid-1959, when the decision to commit Douglas Point was made, the U.K. and the U.S. already had large commercial plants in operation. There was also the prospect of overseas sales for nuclear reactors. The federal government was being urged to get ahead with its 200 megawatt CANDU reactor as quickly as possible so as "not to miss out on the reactor export market."[61]

Canadian prestige was also at stake since nuclear power was the one "game" in which it was felt by some that Canada could compete with the big nations in the international sphere. At the same time there was no assurance of success in the game. In 1956, W.J. Bennett pointed out that "No one can say at this time which type or types of power reactors will prove to be the most economic."[62] This situation was the same four years later when Opposition Leader Mr. Lester Pearson said:

> There has been a great deal of argument as to this form of nuclear power development (i.e., CANDU) versus other forms. I am not qualified to express an opinion ... we must all hope that ... the course on which

we are moving ... will turn out to be the proper one.[63]

Despite the doubts expressed by AECL and the politicians, both wished to push on towards the commercial realization of nuclear power.

One motivation which has been suggested for the government's eagerness was the cancellation in 1959 of the Avro Arrow fighter aircraft project.[64] This was bitterly resented in some quarters and it resulted in the Diefenbaker Government being accused of failing to support a unique (and successful) Canadian high technology endeavour. The haste to push on with CANDU is seen by some as the Government's attempt to redress the adverse image caused by the Arrow cancellation.[65]

Another reason for the rapid development of nuclear power which seems to have influenced some politicians lay in the excess uranium production that was piling up at Canadian mines. The U.S. and U.K. demands for uranium for weapons programs began to fall in the late 1950s and none of the world's nuclear reactor programs were expanding as rapidly as had been foreseen some years previously.[66] As a result, at mines such as Elliot Lake there were slow-downs in production and threats of closure. The Minister of Trade and Commerce, Gordon Churchill, made the point clearly when he stated during a House debate that one of the objectives of the nuclear program was "to expand the civil market, both domestic and foreign for Canadian uranium."[67] This point was re-emphasized the following year during a debate on supply when the government was urged by the opposition to get ahead with CANDU as quickly as possible so that a use could be found for the uranium inventories being built up in Canada, "which was in prospect of closing mines at Elliot Lake."[68]

A final reason for the haste over Douglas Point is the pressure put on the federal government by a provincial crown corporation, Ontario Hydro. It was noted above that Hydro was running out of available hydraulic sites and alternative sources would have to be adopted in the early 1960s. Imported American coal would have to be used to fill part of the gap between Hydro's supply and demand estimates, but the sooner nuclear power was available to help bridge the gap the better.

Whatever weighting is given to the factors described above they were sufficient, cumulatively, to persuade the government that "technological leapfrogging" was justifiable and to go ahead without waiting for NPD to demonstrate that the Canadian nuclear power system was in fact feasible. In the words of one official, the responsible minister, Gordon Churchill, told AECL "to get on with it."

(5) The Douglas Point Decision - A Reversal of Policy

The decision to push ahead with the Douglas Point station was accompanied by a reversal of the policy that Canadian private industry should be responsible for the design and construction of nuclear power stations. This policy had been enunciated many times since the decision to embark on a nuclear power program had been made in 1953. One of the clearest statements was made by C.D. Howe in the House of Commons in 1956. Speaking on behalf of the Government's (and AECL's) operational responsibility towards the development of nuclear power, he stated:

> We stand ready to give advice on design and scientific work that may help any project, but it is not our intention to build such projects, and push them out into various parts of Canada. We simply act as consultants for who-ever wants to go into the business of building atomic power plants.[69]

Howe had been the minister in charge of Canada's atomic energy program since its inception. He was replaced after the Conservatives were elected in 1957 by Gordon Churchill who was appointed chairman of the Privy Council Committee on Scientific and Industrial Research.

The president of AECL, W.J. Bennett, who was also a strong advocate of private sector involvement in the development of nuclear power, resigned as president of AECL on April 30, 1958, and was replaced by J. Lorne Gray.[70] Gray did not have the same commitment to private sector involvement in the nuclear power industry as did his predecessor. His experience with industry had given him a mistrust of its capabilities. Before the House of Commons Special Committee on Research he stated:

> The designer normally refers to engineering handbooks or experience of basic design when facing new problems. However, when he finds that there is nothing in a handbook and the problem is beyond his experience and cannot be solved from basic principles, he talks over possible designs with a manufacturer. This is where Canadian industry falls short. The problems are beyond the normal industrial design office and can only be answered by actually building and testing equipment in an orderly fashion and by employing an experienced development group.[71]

An "experienced development group" was eventually set up by AECL in early 1953 as the Nuclear Power Plant Division, to coordinate the NPD program and direct engineering development on the, as yet uncommitted, large reactor. At the same Committee hearings in 1956 Gray went on to make more scathing comments on the capability of Canadian industry. In referring to AECL's experience in getting components built for the NRU reactor he said:

> The technical problems have been surmounted with no noticeable recognition by [industrial] management of the education value of the exercise.... They give the impression of not wanting to do anything like it again.... Apart from the aircraft and electronics industries there are no experienced development departments in-

Canadian engineering manufacturing companies.[72]

After citing the "branch plant" nature of much of Canadian industry as a reason for these inadequacies, he gave two specific examples of deficiencies which he felt should not have been present in Canadian industry, the lack of first-class welding and of first-class chromium plating. Nonetheless, AECL was trying to encourage industry to improve its performance by providing them with contracts for development work.[73]

AECL's further experience with industry actually undertaking nuclear design and construction was also discouraging. CGE's efforts in the work on NPD left much to be desired in the minds of AECL's management. The cost of NPD was escalating rapidly from the original estimate of $13.5 million, to a figure which was to be eventually $32.8 million.[74] As mentioned above, part of this increase was due to a design change from a pressure vessel to a pressure tube reactor, but part of it was caused by poor cost control on the part of CGE. As an interviewee put it, CGE's cost management was "bloody awful."

This criticism has been accepted by CGE, but it was pointed out in their defence that they had not done any work like this before and by the time NPD was completed their cost management was well under control. The latter point would appear to be true since the other two reactors which CGE was to build, the power reactor in Pakistan and the experimental organic cooled reactor at Whiteshell, were both fixed-price contracts and both were completed on time with a profit to CGE. But these two reactors were in the future. NPD was not to be completed until 1962. In mid-1959 when the decision was being made on Douglas Point, the cost overrun on NPD was being exposed in its worst light.

Another problem with contracting Douglas Point design and construction to industry was the question of which firm could do the job adequately. When CGE formed its design team for NPD, AECL had now re-built and expanded its design team for the initial design work on Douglas Point and there did not seem to be an adequate industrial vehicle to accommodate part of this team even if AECL wanted to. The only candidate was Canadian Westinghouse. Its capability and experience in nuclear design were limited to a study contract provided by AECL in 1958 for the assessment of pressurized light water and boiling light water reactors using enriched fuel as small reactors for use in northern Canada. The Department of Northern Affairs and the Department of National Defence both cooperated in the study, but the conclusion was that they would be too expensive.[75] This limited experience was not enough to persuade AECL that Westinghouse had the necessary staff and competence to design and construct Douglas Point. The decision that AECL was to design and build Douglas Point was greeted with "consternation" at Westinghouse and was later to be subject of a bitter comment by the president of Westinghouse, Mr. William J. Cheeman, before the Lamontagne Committee:

> Again the traditional observation was made that industry does not have the engineers and scientists who can perform the work. However, it is interesting to observe that the same laboratory within two years was able to find the people to grow from 200 to approximately 800 within its own walls.[76]

The laboratory referred to was the Nuclear Power Plant Division of AECL which had to expand considerably to undertake the design and construction of Douglas Point.

In addition to lacking personnel and experience, there would also have been a problem in obtaining an adequate financial committment from a private industrial company. When proposals were called for NPD, CGE had offered to provide $2 million of the expected $13.5 million cost of the plant. Douglas Point was expected to cost $81.5 million. It is doubtful whether any Canadian company could have afforded or could be expected in practical terms to invest in this kind of cost-sharing arrangement, since the Canadian market was so small and uncertain.

The other major factor in the reversal of the government's policy with respect to Douglas Point was Ontario Hydro. As noted above, they were anxious for the program to go ahead quickly in order to provide them with an alternative source of power to American coal. But Hydro had its own views on the design and construction of its power stations. Its preferred solution was to use its own staff for the design of the stations and for negotiating and supervising contracts with equipment suppliers. They had set up teams to do this work for their hydraulic and coal power stations, and were in the process of building up a team, in conjunction with AECL, to do the same for nuclear power stations. One thing they did not want to do was to put themselves in a position where they would have to rely on a single source for any of their requirements. Thus they would not have looked with favour on CGE obtaining the contract for Douglas Point, since this would have given CGE the status as the only supplier of nuclear reactors in Canada.

Also Ontario Hydro did not want to finance the cost of Douglas Point. It would prefer to persuade the federal government to provide financing for the project throught its agent AECL. If AECL were provided the money, Hydro would then prefer that it be expended in a manner which would improve the capability and experience of the joint AECL/Hydro team in Toronto rather than be used by another design and construction team.

(6)   <u>Intervention and Industrial Development</u>

For the reasons described above, the views of AECL and Ontario Hydro were similar. Hence the government's policy with respect to industrial participation in the provision of nuclear power was reversed. The new reactor was of great importance to both parties. For AECL it would be a technical achievement of the first magnitude that would keep Canada abreast of other nuclear power countires. For Ontario Hydro, it was a necessity as an alternative power source, and it would maintain its existing way of contracting new installations. Neither crown corporation felt it could trust industry to do the job adequately, and the pressure from them was successful in getting the previous policy reversed.

Events in other countries would appear to support the wisdom of the decision made in mid-1959. Only in the U.S. has private industry successfully developed and sold nuclear power systems. Even there, several manufacturers have fallen by the wayside after losing considerable sums of money in their nuclear ventures. GE and Westinghouse are the only companies remaining as complete nuclear steam supply system manufacturers. These two companies had the combination of foresight and luck to develop good reactor systems, but above all, they had financial resources to carry them through to commercial realization.

In the U.K., after the first two government-financed stations at Calder Hall, a number of consortia of industrial firms were set up for the construction of additional power stations. Because of a lack of orders, domestically and from the export market, they have now been disbanded. In France, construction was at first undertaken by the state, and then when the domestically developed system proved inadequate, a government-dominated company, Framatome, was set up to build Westinghouse reactors under license. In Canada, AECL was to continue to provide the design and development expertise for nuclear power. After NPD came into operation in 1962, the Nuclear Power Plant Division began design of a 500 megawatt station "two of which would comprise the initial stage of a projected four-unit station."[77] In 1964 the decision to build had been made and cost-sharing arrangements had been agreed upon. The station would be located at Pickering, Ontario and when completed would be the largest nuclear power station operating anywhere in the world. The first of the two initial units was scheduled for completion in late 1970 and the second a year later.

In making the announcement in the House, Mr. Drury, Minister of Industry, pointed out that committing a very large nuclear power station at this relatively early stage in nuclear development produced considerable financial risks which made participation by governments desirable. The estimated cost of the station would be $226 million and contributions from Ontario Hydro and the provincial and federal governments would be made as follows:

> Ontario Hydro will be responsible for an amount equal to the cost of a coal-burning power station of the same capacity they are building at Lampton, estimated to be $120 million. The balance will be subscribed by the two governments in the ratio of 1.2 to 1 with the Federal government advancing the larger portion. In terms of the present estimates of cost the federal government will subscribe $79.5 million and the Ontario government $66.5 million. It is anticipated that the capital advanced by the parties will be fully repaid with interest at normal rates out of the operating revenues of the station. There is a good possibility of profit in government investments and reduced costs in the production of power.[78]

The financial commitment by Ontario Hydro is similar to the one made in the case of Douglas Point where the utility offered to purchase the reactor for a sum equal to the cost of a comparable coal-fired station. The commitment by the federal government in support of this first, still experimental, station is considerably less than the offer of 50 percent loan financing which is now being made to provincial utilities proposing to erect nuclear power stations.

With hindsight, the Canadian decision to concentrate nuclear power design and development in AECL seems to have been, but was not necessarily, inevitable. Canadian industry did not have the financial resources necessary to maintain design and development teams and facilities during years of uncertain reactors sales and were given little incentive to do so. The one company which attempted it, CGE, eventually in 1968 merged its nuclear team with that of AECL. Despite the comments of their president in 1970, Westinghouse is probably glad now that it did not press to become a member of Canada's nuclear reactor club in 1959.

Today, the Ontario nuclear power program is large enough to justify Ontario Hydro supporting its own nuclear design team, using AECL expertise as required on a consulting basis.[79] All other reactors, whether in Canada or overseas, are being provided by AECL through its newly created Atomic Energy of Canada Engineering Company.[80]

Government intervention in the nuclear industry was first propelled by the compelling requirements of war time security and the race to produce nuclear weapons. Economic ideology was not itself a factor. In the early 1950s, when AECL was created it was a policy objective to reduce the total proportion of public sector involvement. This stance seemed in part to be based on ideology, but not blatantly so. This objective was confronted by the constraints of foreign ownership of the only two corporations capable of participating, but whose parent firms were then evolving into the core of American industry with a different reactor to sell. The choice, in part, seemed to be to create from these industrial fragments either a single private "monopoly" instrument of policy or a public one. Since Ontario Hydro (the major buyer of the power generated) already was in existence, it was unwilling to be placed in a dependent position where its control would be threatened. Intervention was also propelled by a strong willingness to express faith in technology and technologists.

The reactor case study raises two further interesting questions about intervention. First, it shows that the prime beneficiary of federal public enterprise and of federal subsidies was Ontario Hydro, the Ontario Government and the Ontario taxpayer. It is difficult to explain how Ontario benefitted so much without having to share much of the overhead developmental costs. Technical personnel at Ontario Hydro did share the technical risks. Indeed, the AECL-Hydro partnership seems to be best explained by the sense of technological adventure. In this sense, there was some shared risk. In purely financial terms, the federal government bore most of the risks and Ontario gladly reaped the benefits, especially in the early developmental phases.

Another aspect of intervention raised by the case is the possible substitutability of policy instruments. While the analysis has shown why AECL and Ontario Hydro increasingly assumed the direct contractor, engineering and design role, one is still entitled to raise the question in hindsight of whether the effect on the subsequent development of CANDU would have been different had both AECL and Ontario Hydro decided to use a private firm like CGE as their chosen instrument. Instead of intervention through direct public ownerhsip there would have been a higher proportion of intervention through the instrument of contracts. Contracting out a far larger proportion of the engineering and design may have produced a stiffer market test for the viability of nuclear power. It also might have brought out into the open certain transactions which otherwise were carried out within a Crown corporation.

The point to be stressed here is not that results would have automatically been different if a different instrument had been used but that a failure to consider such alternatives and the possible substitutability of instruments can affect future choices in industrial development.

NOTES: Chapter 6

1. Margaret Gowing, <u>Independence and Deterence, Britain and Atomic Energy, 1945-52, Vol. I, Policy Making</u> (London: The Macmillan Press Ltd., 1974), p. 54.

2. For a layman's description of the general aspects of nuclear reactors design, see S. Glasstone, <u>Sourcebook on Atomic Energy</u>, (Princeton, New Jersey: D. von Rostrand, 1958), p. 449, et. seq.

3. W.B. Lewis, "An Atomic Power Proposal," August 27, 1951. It was later published as AECL 186 in 1956.

4. See Richard G. Hewlett and Oscar E. Anderson, <u>A History of the United States Atomic Energy Commission: The New World 1939-46</u> (Pittsburgh: Pennsylvania State University Press, 1962), Vol. I.

5. See W.H. Zinn, F.K. Pittman and J.F. Hogerton, <u>Nuclear Power USA</u> (New York: McGraw-Hill, 1966); and Richard G. Hewlett and Francis Duncan <u>Nuclear Navy 1946-62</u> (Chicago: University of Chicago Press, 1976).

6. Peter de Leon, <u>A Cross National Comparison of Nuclear Development Strategies</u>, (Santa Monica: RAND Corporation, October 1976), p. 10.

7. Appropriately, the Shippingport reactor went critical on December 2, 1957, the fifteenth anniversary of the first nuclear chain reaction in the reactor at Chicago; see Samuel Glasstone, <u>Sourcebook on Atomic Energy</u>, op. cit., p. 467.

8. Grave doubts have been expressed concerning the accuracy of this estimated cost and of subsequent estimated costs for LWRs. See Irwin C. Bupp and Jean-Claude Derian, <u>Light Water</u> (New York: Basic Books, 1978).

9. Peter de Leon, op. cit., p. 14.

10. R.W. Roberts, <u>Fission Technology</u>, Third Energy Technology Conference, 1976, p. 29.

11. See Margaret Gowing, <u>Independence and Deterrence</u> ... Vol. I, Policy Making, op. cit.

12. Ibid., p. 228.

13. Margaret Gowing, <u>Independence and Deterrence, Britain and Atomic Energy, 1945-52, Vol. II, Policy Execution</u> (London: The Macmillan Press Ltd., 1974), p. 262.

14. Sir Christopher Hinton, "The Graphite Moderated Gas Cooled Pile," <u>Proceedings of the International Conference on the Peaceful Uses of Atomic Energy</u>, Vol. III. Power Reactors. (New York: United Nations, 1955), p. 322.

15. J.W. Kendall and T.M. Fry, "The Downreay Fast Reactor Project," <u>Proceedings of the International Conference on the Peaceful Uses of Atomic Energy</u>, Vol. 3 (New York: United Nations, 1955), p. 193.

16. "The Role of Nuclear Power in Ontario," Submissions to the Royal Commission on Electric Power Planning, Canadian Nuclear Association, August 1976, p. A2-1.

17. Peter de Leon, <u>op. cit.</u>, p. 20.

18. Central Electricity Generating Board, <u>An Assessment of the Technical and Economic Aspects of Dungeness 'B' Nuclear Power Station</u>, London, July 1965, p. 2.

19. Laurence Scheinman, <u>Atomic Energy in France Under the Fourth Republic</u> (Princeton: Princeton University Press, 1965), p. 211.

20. P. Chambadal and M. Pascal, "Recovery of the Energy Produced in an Air-Cooled Graphite Reactor G 1," <u>Proceedings of the International Conference on the Peaceful Uses of Atomic Energy</u>, Vol. 3 (New York: United Nations, 1955), p. 81.

21. P.P. Ailleret, et al., "Design for a Dual Purpose Reactor," <u>Proceedings of the International Conference on the Peaceful Uses of Atomic Energy</u>, Vol. 3 (New York: United Nations, 1955).

22. Peter de Leon, <u>op. cit.</u>, p. 29.

23. <u>Ibid.</u>, p. 31.

24. See Bupp and Derian, <u>op. cit.</u>, Chapter 4.

25. See A.M. Petrostants, *From Scientific Search to Atomic Industry* (Daville, Ill.: The Interstate Press, 1975), p. 93.

26. D.I. Blokhintsev and N.A. Nikileav, "The First Atomic Power Station in the U.S.S.R.," *Proceedings of the International Conference on the Peaceful Uses of Atomic Energy*, Vol. 3 (New York: United Nations, 1955), p. 55.

27. Peter de Leon, *op. cit.*, p. 15.

28. *Ibid.*, p. 18.

29. This includes Russian reactor exports to Finland which as we will see played an indirect role in the development of Canada's reactor export program.

30. House of Commons Special Committee on Research (HCSCR). *Minutes and Proceedings of Evidence*, No. 11, 3 July 1956, p. 389. Giving evidence before the committee Mr. W.J. Bennett said AECL expenditures would be about $160 million for the next five years. Appropriations for the same period would be $110-$115 million. This would suggest revenues of $45-$50 million over the five year period. A reactor loop is a large tube passing through the reactor core which can contain large reactor experiments (such as the new fuel designs or types) and their associated equipment. When NRX was put out of commission by an accident in 1952, the U.S. Navy sent train loads of sailors to Chalk River to help in the clean-up operations because some experiments crucial to their new pressurized water submarine reactor were being conducted in NRX loops.

31. *Ibid.*, p. 2013.

32. *Ibid.*, p. 2017.

34. House of Commons, *Debates*, Session 1953-54, 2 June 1954, p. 5403.

35. AECL, Annual Report, 1953-54, p. 4.

36. HCSCR, No. 1, 30 April 1956, p. 277.

37. AECL, Annual Report, 1953-54, p. 5.

38. For a more complete statement of AECL's policy at this time see W.J. Bennett, "Statement on Canadian Atomic Energy Program," AECL 168, 1955.

39. The insistence on industrial involvement was in accord with the free enterprise conviction of AECL President, W.J. Bennett, who was also President of Eldorado Mining and Refining Ltd. Questions were asked in the House about his concurrent directorship of Investors Mutual of Canada Ltd., a firm which held stocks in uranium mines. (House of Commons, Debates, Session 1957, 12 April 1957, p. 3437).

40. HCSCR, No. 7, 30 June, 1957, p. 175.

41. GE (USA) was building the prototype boiling light water reactor at Dresden which was in operation in 1954. See "The Role of Nuclear Power in Ontario," Canadian Nuclear Association, August 1976, p. A2-4.

42. House of Commons, Debates, Session 1959, 16 July 1959, p. 6158.

43. For a comprehensive summary of the status of electric power in Canada at that time, see J. David, "Electric Power in Canada," Proceedings of the International Conference on the Peaceful Uses of Atomic Energy, Vol. 3 (New York: United Nations, 1955), p. 166.

44. House of Commons, Debates, Session 1959, 16 July 1959, p. 6158.

45. AECL, Annual Report, 1960-61, p. 9.

46. AECL, Annual Report, 1955-56, p. 5.

- 125 -

47. AECL, Annual Report, 1954-54, p. 5.

48. House of Commons, Debates, Session 1965, 1 March 1956, p. 1699.

49. J.A.L. Robertson, "The Canadian Reactor System," Science, Vol. 199, 1977, p. 657.

50. By the time it was decided to change from the pressure vessel to the pressure tube design, the pressure vessel had already been ordered from Babcock and Wilcox Co., in Renfrew, Scotland. This order was paid for upon cancellation, and as one interviewee put it, "For all we know, it is still there."

51. AECL, Annual Report, 1953-54, p. 5.

52. AECL, Annual Report, 1957-58, p. 7.

53. House of Commons, Debates Session 1957-58, 1 February 1958, p. 4147.

54. Ibid., p. 4147.

55. AECL, Annual Report, 1959-60, p. 7.

56. House of Commons, Debates, Session 1959, 18 June 1959, p. 4862.

57. AECL, Annual Report, 1959-60, p. 6.

58. AECL, Annual Report, 1968-69, p. 6.

59. AECL, Annual Report, 1977-78, p. F11.

60. AECL, Annual Report, 1976-77, p. F10.

61. House of Commons, Debates, Session 1959, 16 July 1959, p. 6117.

62. HCSCR, No. 1, 30 April 1965, p. 239.

63. House of Commons, Debates, Session 1960, 10 August 1960, p. 7903.

64. James Dow, The Arrow (Toronto: Lorimer and Co., 1979).

65. This point of view was suggested at interviews.

66. G.M. MacNabb, "Nuclear and Uranium Policies," Canadian Nuclear Association Annual Conference, 1975, p. 20.

67. House of Commons, Debates, Session 1958, 3 September 1958.

68. House of Commons, Debates, Session 1959, 16 July 1959, p. 6117.

69. House of Commons, Debates, Session 1956, 5 August 1956, p. 7317.

70. AECL, Annual Report, 1957-58, p. 20.

71. HCSCR, No. 1, 30 April 1956, p. 255.

72. Ibid., p. 256.

73. Ibid., p. 257.

74. House of Commons, Debates, Session 1962-63, 5 November 1963, p. 1284.

75. AECL, Annual Report, 1960-61, p. 13.

76. Report of the Senate Special Committee on Science Policy, Vol. 1, p. 239 (Ottawa: Queen's Printer, 1970).

77. AECL, Annual Report, 1963-64, p. 11.

78. House of Commons, Debates, Session 1964, 20 August 1964, p. 7051.

79. AECL, Annual Report, 1964-65, p. 7.

80. AECL, News Release, 28 July, 1978.

Chapter 7

Intervention, Technology and Regulation: The Uranium Miners Case*

The focus of most of the current controversies about the role and regulation of nuclear power has been on the middle and "back end" of the nuclear fuel cycle. The safety of nuclear power plants and, more recently, the problems of nuclear waste management and fuel reprocessing have received the major share of scientific and political attention. This chapter focusses on issues at the "front end" of the nuclear fuel cycle, the regulation of the health of Canadian uranium miners by the federal Atomic Energy Control Board (AECB) and the Ontario provincial regulatory authorities.

The Ontario Royal Commission on the Health and Safety of Workers in Mines (the Ham Commission) has shown conclusively that uranium miners have paid a heavy price for past regulatory inadequacy. It concluded that "as at the end of 1974, lung cancer deaths [of uranium workers] were in significant excess by a total of 36 cases or 80 percent of the expected deaths."[1]

The chapter will, in particular, relate a number of aspects of the role of science and technology outlined in Chapter 4 to recent regulatory intervention or the lack thereof in the nuclear industry. These aspects include Hafele's concept of "hypotheticality" in the nuclear power debate; the openness of

---

* This chapter is adapted from the author's earlier article published in <u>Canadian Public Administration</u>, Vol. 21 (Spring 1978), pp. 51-82. The permission of the Institute of Public Administration of Canada to adapt the article is gratefully acknowledged.

the regulatory process; the relationships between causal knowledge and political perception; the relationship between the regulators' research priorities and the lack of applied controls and monitoring technology; the degree of deference paid by domestic regulators to international standard-setting bodies; and finally the redistributive effects encouraged by a lack of appropriate science and technology priorities.

Regulatory behaviour and the effectiveness of regulatory activity are ultimately determined by the larger variables in the nuclear political economy examined in Chapter 2 and 3. The uranium miners case illustrates the need to understand the role of science and technology in the regulatory process and in government intervention. Regulatory intervention is affected by the full spectrum of scientific and technological activity including the acquisition, analysis and publication of data, the pursuit of pure research (or the search for causal knowledge), the adoption and adaptation of applied production technologies, and the development and deployment of applied technologies to monitor exposures in the workplace. Regulation is therefore dependent upon the existence of scientific and technological personnel in the applied as well as the pure science fields and by the way in which new research is received and communicated by regulators and their advisors.

Because the analysis deals with a case study it must be examined with all the usual caveats about the limitations of case studies. Other case studies are available, however, which tend to show that the regulatory inadequacies demonstrated by the uranium miners case are not unique.[2] There are, moreover, pressing practical reasons why some "lessons" about the uranium miners' case should not be lost sight of. This urgency arises out of the fact that the uranium industry is in the midst of an economic boom in which important crown enterprises, federal and provincial, have a direct stake. It was in an earlier boom twenty years ago that the political and economics seeds of regulatory inadequacy were sown, soon to be reinforced by the more specific role of science and technology in the nuclear regulatory process. A grossly disproportionate share of the costs of past regulatory inadequacy was born by the uranium miners.

This chapter is organized in four sections. The first section will provide a brief but somewhat more detailed profile than provided in Chapter 2 of the economic climate within which the regulation of the health of uranium miners occurred particularly in the 1950s and 1960s. The second section will present a brief but also more detailed background profile than that surveyed in Chapter 4 of the main operating habits of the federal and Ontario regulatory authorities. Section three will then focus on the determination of exposure standards and on the processes created to ensure compliance with those standards. Finally we will offer observations about regulatory intervention with the focus on those aspects of science and technology listed above and outlined in Chapter 4.

(1) The Economic Climate for Regulation

The uranium industry has been characterized by widely fluctuating periods of economic activity. Between 1954 and 1958 a dozen mines were rushed into production in the Elliot Lake region and four more in the Bancroft region, primarily to meet American contracts. The regulatory environment was thus characterized by pressures which resulted in some short cuts being taken. Then the uranium industry almost collapsed when markets declined rapidly in the late 1950s and early 1960s. By 1961 all but three mines had closed.[3] An executive of Denison Mines told the Ham Commission that in the early expansion years the attainment of safety was "a desperate and difficult task."[4] He attributed difficulties to the short-time demands for orders, a severe shortage of skilled miners, new ore body characteristics, and the state of worker attitudes in a boom town which was not conducive to safety.[5] Employment in Elliot Lake rose from 500 in 1954 to 10,000 at the end of 1958. By 1962 it was below 3,000 and by the mid-1970s, despite improving demand for uranium, employment remained at only 1600.[6]

A second and partly related characteristic of the regulatory and industrial environment is that a significant number of foreign and migrant workers were employed in the uranium mines. Thus, the perceived impact on Canadian labour and labour unions was also temporary and subject to wide fluctuations in interest. Labour unions in the uranium mining industry have always expressed great concern about working conditions, but they have not uniformly and persistently pressed the issue given the periods of instability in the uranium industry.[7]

It is also important to stress that it was a federal crown agency, Eldorado Nuclear Ltd. (then known as Eldorado Mining and Refining Limited) which was the sole purchaser of uranium oxide and other nuclear materials and which entered into the contracts with the Ontario mines. The president of Eldorado Nuclear was a member of the AECB, the federal regulatory authority.[8]

The views of the main uranium mining companies about the evolution of their industry and its consequences on the health of miners were clearly revealed in the Ham Commission hearings. An executive of Rio Algom Ltd. stressed concern about possible radical departures in the principles of compensation because it could be concluded that anybody who worked in the uranium mines and suffered from cancer would be a compensable charge against the industry when there may be no causal connection. He felt such compensation should be charged to the public treasury.[9] Similarly, spokesmen for Denison Mines stressed the technical difficulty of monitoring exposures.[10]

Finally, it is important to stress that during the 1958 to 1974 period, mining companies were carrying out regular quarterly and semi-annual dust and radiation surveys. These records were transmitted partly through the Mine Accident Prevention Association (MAPAO) to the Ministry of Natural Resources. These readings were not made public until the research staff of Ontario Opposition Leader Stephen Lewis obtained them in 1974. After analysis, he revealed to the Ham Commission, that "in not a single instance did the average underground dust counts for the uranium mines of Elliot Lake ever fall below the recommended limits"[11] suggested by MAPAO.

(2) The Regulatory Authorities

We have already outlined in Chapter 5, the central statutory mandate conferred on the federal AECB by the Atomic Energy Control Act and the regulations made pursuant to it. We also outlined the federal-provincial administrative accommodation regarding inspection and compliance in mine safety. To understand the uranium miners case, however, it is necessary to understand the structure and evolution of the AECB and of the particular features of the Ontario regulatory apparatus in the 1950s, 1960s and 1970s. We will present a profile of each in turn.

(a) The Atomic Energy Control Board

The AECB consists of one full-time and four part-time members, but it relies heavily on an elaborate network of advisory committees. Typically these committees consists of individual experts and representatives of federal, provincial and some municipal departments and agencies. There are basically three types of committees: safety advisory committees (SACs), technical advisory committees (TACs) and grant advisory committees (GACs).[12] The committees bring to the AECB a diverse range of expertise on nuclear design, health and safety, and nuclear research.

While the committees have no statutory basis, many have virtually de facto decision-making roles in that an adverse judgement by the committee would probably mean that certain proposals would not be approved by the AECB. This is particularly the case for the Reactor Safety Advisory Committee, RSAC (for Ontario, Quebec and New Brunswick). No approval of site, construction, or operation has been given by the AECB without a positive recommendation from the relevant RSAC. Other committees may be created in response to a particular need for regulation-making advice. In 1974 a Mine Safety Advisory Committee was created to advise on safety aspects of uranium and thorium mining and milling operations.

The use of the advisory committee undoubtedly has many advantages for the AECB. It facilitates intergovernmental representation, and gives the board access to scarce expertise. As an organization of scientists and engineers, it is a mechanism which parallels the committee approach developed over the years by the National Research Council (NRC). In professional terms it is a process of peer-group analysis and assessment. Thus far, the concept of representativeness on these committees has not been extended to other constituencies such as labour unions. A serious question arises as to whether the cumulative effect of the use of committees, when coupled with the small size of the AECB staff, has left the board in a vulnerable and excessively dependent position. These issues are always a question of balance, and trade-offs, but the advisory committee process constitutes an important element of the AECB organization. Ultimately, advisory committee members are hidden, part-time staff members of AECB.

The AECB must now interact with a wide range of clientele groups and organizations.[13] These include the nuclear industry (the large state enterprises and the smaller nuclear parts and components industry), other federal departments, provincial and municipal departments, international agencies (particularly the International Atomic Energy Agency), public interest groups and unions. The AECB was conceived in a postwar ear in which the dominant concern was strategic security of atomic energy. The Canadian nuclear community was basically a very small <u>governmental</u> community, confined to NRC and later AECL. The regulatory apparatus was, and probably had to be, a closed professional shop. The membership of the board, and the career patterns of its staff, reinforced and reflected this closed shop. All presidents except for the incumbent came to the Board after long careers in AECL. The presidents of AECL and Eldorado Nuclear have been board members for most of its history.[14] As the nuclear community expanded from AECL into Ontario Hydro, and into physics departments of Canadian universities, a position was reached, probably in the early 1960s, when these closed-shop characteristics need not have existed.[15] The security environment had moderated and the nuclear community was a sufficient size that the Board could have been composed of a much higher proportion of non-governmental agency representatives and experts. In fact, the closed-shop characteristics did not really begin to break down until the early and mid-1970s. It was also only in the 1970s after the success of the Pickering reactors that the CANDU nuclear program began to have any hope of eventually achieving viability.

The AECB has thus had to evolve from a position where it was a combination of a regulator in the interests of security and a benevolent patron of nuclear research in Canadian universities, to a position where it must assume both the appearance and substance of an independent regulator. Such independence is never absolute, but it is now recognized that it can certainly be sought with greater vigour than the AECB has demonstrated, historically speaking. All regulatory boards in the Canadian system of parliamentary responsible government are dependent upon some ministerial and cabinet authority and power.[16] While standards are set by the Board, all boards tend to rely to a significant extent on the detailed "front-line" requirements developed by and carried out by the utilities or industries or sectors they are regulating. All boards must secure the cooperation of a host of other governmental agencies to effectively carry out their tasks. The question of independence is clearly one of degree, but the burden of evidence indicates that the AECB, despite recent movements in this direction, has not nearly achieved the appropriate degree of independence.

Every organization develops its own standard operating habits. It needs such habits largely to help it pursue goals and also to reduce the areas of uncertainty as presented both by its statutory and policy mandate and by its organizational environment. An examination of these habits helps tell us how the organization perceives and defines its own roles.

Several observations about the AECB's standard operating habits are important in this regard.

First, in general terms, the Board has historically perceived its constituency to be primarily the utilities, other government departments, and nuclear experts. From 1970 to 1974 AECB embarked upon a major comprehensive revision and consolidation of its regulations. This was a major regulation-making and review exercise but it was carried out largely within the confines of its traditional habits and constituencies.[17] Little thought was given to holding broader public hearings or meetings, despite the fact that nuclear issues were already of growing concern, despite the use of such consultative processes by other regulatory authorities such as the CRTC, and despite the fact that the Board has the power to change procedures of this kind. The Board has relied on its advisory committee process almost exclusively as a device for intergovernmental representation and expert (peer-group) representation but for no other form of representation.

Secondly, if one examines only the budgets of the AECB, in the absence of other information, one would be forced to conclude that the AECB was primarily a benevolent patron of the basic nuclear physics research community in Canada.[18] About 80 percent of the AECB's budget have gone to its basic research-oriented granting program. It is this function which has contributed greatly to the board's historic image of being a promoter of the industry. This exists despite the fact that the disposition of the granting budget takes scarcely a few days of the Board's time. The remainder is taken up with its regulatory functions on which the other 20 percent of its budget is spent. It is also this research policy bias which has contributed to the relative lack of attention given to the front end of the nuclear fuel cycle where the occupational costs are being borne by uranium miners.

(b) <u>The Ontario Regulatory Agencies</u>

While the AECB had clear legal jurisdiction to regulate almost all aspects of the industry, Chapter 4 has shown that administrative arrangements were made with provincial authorities. Since most uranium mining has been concentrated in Ontario, it is the Ontario administrative response that is most essential to understand. This response is primarily conditioned by the one-party (Progressive Conservative) dominance over the past three decades, and by the self-regulatory mode of operation between the government and the mining industry. The latter is enshrined in the <u>Mining Act</u>.[19] It places responsibility for health and safety on mine management. The Ministry of Natural Resources provides the main inspection capability for mining safety generally through the Mines Engineering Branch. The latter is composed almost entirely of professional engineers.

In testimony before the Ontario Royal Commission on the Health and Safety of Workers in Mines (Ham Commission), the Minister of Natural Resources, Leo Bernier, while acknowledging that unions have a lack of confidence in the Mines Engineering Branch, nonetheless asserted that "the basic self-regulating system we have here in Ontario is a good and workable system."[20] Other testimony by the deputy minister of the ministry stressed that the self-regulatory approach enabled the ministry to adopt a "pre-engineering" rather than a "traffic cop" approach to regulation.[21]

The Ontario Ministry of Health, through its Occupational Health Protection Branch, provides assistance on request to the Ministry of Natural Resources (and other departments). The deputy minister of health stated before the Ham Commission that the ministry "does not take the place of factory or mining inspection but assists these jurisdictions in special problems that require a research approach."[22]

The Workmens' Compensation Board (WCB) is important not only because it provides compensation to workers, but also because, through its levies on employers, it funds the Mines Accident Prevention Association of Ontario (MAPAO). MAPAO shares the services of the same executive director as the Ontario Mining Association, an industrial association which pressed for the creation of MAPAO, before the latter was formed in 1930.[23]

The Workmens' Compensation Board was initially created to compensate victims of industrial accidents and to encourage better safety practices through processes that were less burdened by either the procedural complexity and costs of the regular courts, or by the perceived prejudicial, or at least unsympathetic attitude of judges toward workers. The WCB contains representation from industry and the compensation is based on direct industrial levies. The levies on industry change according to a particular industry or firm's safety record over time. The WCB was also intended, in part at least, to take some of the burden of proof for compensable claims away from workers both as a matter of operating philosphy and through the investigative role of the WCB staff.

The WCB has developed a generally effective method of operation for their traditional areas of concern, namely industrial safety. With respect to industrial health and toxic substances, however, the board has been less successful. First, the WCB has suffered from the normal hardening of the organizational arteries that seem to afflict all mature organizations that have developed some success in their traditional operating areas. Secondly, the WCB has been among the first to have to deal with specific cases of silicosis and cancer of uranium miners. Because of our past social failure at preventing occupational diseases, the WCB is brought to the centre of the debate about the nature and adequacy of causal knowledge and evidence referred to above. On the one hand, the WCB feels that it cannot give compensation merely because a few claimants, or even their doctors, think their illness was caused by a toxic substance in the workplace. On the other hand, the tradition of the WCB is supposed to give the benefit of the doubt to the worker and so to lessen the burden of proof on the worker.

Canadian WCBs are thus properly under enormous pressures. The British Columbia board has recently been under pressure from industry for being too generous to labour, and the Ontario board has been the object of persistent and rigorous criticism by the NDP leader, Stephen Lewis, for being insensitive to labour claimants. It is clear that health hazards created by uranium greatly increase the nature of the regulatory stakes. For industry the issue is no longer just fixing a guardrail, but rather involves potentially new, often expensive, production technologies. This in turn can be related to corporate safety and health records and the industrial levies from which WCBs derive their revenue. In short, the politics, economics, and organization of the regulatory process are inextricably and closely linked.

Finally it should be noted that the Ontario WCB has custody of the Nominal Roll of Uranium Miners. This role was developed very gradually as suspicions about the link between lung cancer and uranium mining emerged in the late 1960s, particularly after exploratory searches for causes of death among uranium miners in Ontario records of vital statistics.[24] The Ham Commission stressed that none of these early suspicions by Health and WCB experts were communicated to workers or to their unions although they were communicated through mines inspectors to mine management.[25]

(3) The Determination of Exposure Standards and Compliance Practices

The health of uranium miners has been seriously harmed both by silicosis and by lung cancer caused by ionizing radiation.[26] While this section focuses more on the latter, the relationship between science and technology and the derivation of regulatory standards and of monitoring and compliance practices in both occupational diseases is important. A brief account of the standard-setting and compliance processes will thus be presented, with the focus on radiation hazards.

The Ontario authorities accepted in 1958 the then generally recommended international standard of One Working Level (1.0 WL) for the maximum permissable concentration of radium and its daughters in air set by the International Commission on Radiological Protection (ICRP) and also adopted by the U.S. Public Health Service. The guidelines, however, had no statutory significance. Between 1955 and 1958 no auditing of mines took place and hence by far the worst radiation-conditions existed during this rapid period of expansion.[27]

Following a 1959 revised ICRP recommendation of 0.3 WL, the Ontario Mines and Health departments met in 1960 to review the ICRP recommendation and to assess the difficulty the Ontario uranium mines were having in reaching the generally accepted target of 1.0 WL. Experts from AECL's Chalk River Nuclear Laboratories and the U.S. Public Health Service were invited to the meeting to give their views on these matters, but the AECB was not consulted on this occasion. The meeting produced a consensus that the ICRP recommendation of the equivalent of 0.3 WL should be adopted as a target to be attained within the next five years.[28] In fact, by 1967 the 1960 consensus had not been implemented. Interested Ontario authorities adopted as a guideline the American standard of 12 Working Level Months (WLM) per annum.[29]

By 1964, only three uranium mines remained in operation in the Elliot Lake area. Although Rio Algom (Nordic) had substantially reduced radon daughter concentrations in its mines, the AECB was concerned about the continuing high levels that existed in the Denison and Stanrock mines. While formal reports on radiation levels had not been received by AECB, its president, based on other information, visited these two mines to emphasize the Board's concern.

In the late 1960s, both internal Ontario evidence as well as American evidence began to show an excess risk of lung cancer among uranium miners. The American evidence came from a U.S. Public Health Service study published in 1967 and resulted in the Americans adopting an <u>enforceable standard</u> of 1.0 WL.[34] In response to the U.S. study a meeting was held in mid-1967 attended by officers of the AECB, the Ontario authorities, and experts from the Department of National Health and Welfare (DNH&W) and AECL. At this meeting, the AECL expert expressed his concern over concentrations prevailing in the Canadian mines, re-emphasized his belief that the 1960 decision to work towards the ICRP recommendation of the equivalent of 0.3 WL was correct, and recommended that as an immediate step the regulatory authorities should insist on all mines meeting a 1.0 WL requirement. This meeting of officers and experts was followed by a visit to the Elliot Lake area by those who attended the meeting, to discuss the problem with officials of the three operating mines. The mining companies outlined their plans for reducing the concentrations in their mines and it was believed by AECB officials that further improvement was possible through their efforts.

Following the 1967 meeting, the president of the AECB wrote to the deputy minister of the Ontario Department of Mines to state that the Board viewed the radon daughter problem very seriously and urged the department to require the mines to improve the situation. At the request of the mines' representative attending the 1967 meeting, the president of the AECB recommended to the federal Department of Energy, Mines and Resources that a radiation instrument calibration facility be established at the department's mining research laboratory at Elliot Lake. The calibration facility was established in 1968.

Late in 1967 the chief engineer of mines of the Ontario Department of Mines issued a mine order requiring occupational exposure to radon daughters in Ontario mines to be controlled to 12 Working Level Months (WLM) per year. In 1972, the control level was reduced to 8 WLM for 1973 and 6 WLM for 1974, and in 1974 the control level was further reduced to 4 WLM for 1975.

The AECB's brief to the Ham Commission pointed out that in 1969 an AECB officer, accompanied by officers of the Ontario Departments of Mines and Health, met with representatives of Denison Mines to review progress in controlling the radon daughter hazard. At that time 90 to 95 percent of the mine working areas were at concentrations below 1.0 WL and over the year ending July 1969, only nine out of 417 underground workers had received over 12 WLM exposure. The majority had received less than 6 WLM exposure. An officer of the AECB visited Rio Algom (Quirke) and Denison again in 1971 and noted that progress was being made in reducing radon daughter levels.

Documents produced before the Ham Commission showed, however, that the Ontario authorities had other information that ought to have raised more visible concern. Correspondence dated February 19, 1969 between Mr. W.C. Wheeler of the WCB and Dr. Sutherland, then Chief of Occupational Health in the Ministry of Health, showed cancer-related causes in 16 of 20 deaths of uranium miners identified in the letters.[31] Neither the contents nor the possible implications of this information were passed on either publicly or privately to the unions.

Ontario authorities, as noted above, began to lower the standards by 1973 and also in that year prohibited smoking in uranium mines. They had also begun the development of the Nominal Roll. Generally, however, they waited until 1974 before publicly acknowledging the magnitude of the problem through the publication of the Muller-Wheeler report,[32] which showed the excess risk of uranium miners. Criticism was levelled by the unions for releasing the report through the forum of an international scientific conference in Bordeaux, France in September 1974 rather than more directly to the workers most affected.[33]

Following the issuance in June 1974 of the revised Atomic Energy Control Regulations, the AECB, in November 1974, reviewed its procedure for licensing of uranium mines and established the Mine Safety Advisory Committee. This committee, which includes experts from appropriate federal and provincial departments, has the mandate to consider related health and safety aspects and recommend conditions for licensing purposes. The Committee is also expected to make recommendations to the Board with regard to the adoption of appropriate health and safety standards. Under the revised AECB regulations of 1974, applicants for mining licences are required to submit pre-licensing safety reports describing:

a) the procedures and equipment to be used to mine and mill the ore and to manage the waste products that are generated in these operations; and

b) the measures to be taken under routine and a normal operating conditions to protect the health and safety of workers, and members of the public who may be affected by the proposed operations.[34]

This information is considered by the Mine Safety Advisory Committee which specifies conditions as required for licensing purposes. When milling operations have commenced, licensees are now required to submit periodic reports to include:

a) summaries of radiation and dust counts in the mine and mill and employee exposures to these contaminants;

b) a record of the amounts of contaminant released to the environment;

c) a description of any unusual occurrences that may have affected the health and safety of the workers or members of the public; and

d) a description of any changes in procedures or equipment that may effect the safety of the operations.[35]

This information is reviewed by the Board staff and the Mine Safety Advisory Committee as appropriate.

The AECB has stressed that its past regulatory involvement in uranium mines both in degree and nature was developed in response to government policy directions. Thus it noted that,

The dominant policy direction was to make administrative arrangements whereby the provincial agencies were asked to be operationally responsible for health and safety under their regulations and the federal government, through AECB, asserted its control in licensing for purposes of security control over the disposition of ores and concentrates. During the past 20 years or more, there has been continuous pressure from the provinces to place all aspects of the control of uranium mines completely under provincial jurisdiction with no federal involvement. The annual Mines Ministers Conference have repeatedly urged the federal government to vacate the uranium mining field but the senior level of government refused and maintained a position of cooperative control.[36]

Current AECB policy seeks to ensure that the AECB can be more directly involved in ensuring that fully effective measures are implemented to protect the health of miners. It more candidly acknowledges that its heretofore advisory interventions have had limited impact because of the overall division of responsibility under former policy guidelines.

The Board has also changed its research priorities. Its granting program, as noted earlier, had been almost exclusively oriented to the support of basic high energy physics in Canadian universities. While logical in some respects in the early years, this research priority also served to informally co-opt the one pool of expertise in universities who could have acted as critics of the AECB. The Board has begun to develop its research role in more applied directions, so as to support its regulatory and compliance functions. This includes work on mine tailings and on monitoring technology.

The most recent, and by far the most open phase of the regulatory process, has been the Ham Commission itself. The Commission was established in 1975 as a response by the Ontario Conservative government to the tenacious criticism, in a situation of minority government, of the Ministry of Natural Resources by Stephen Lewis, Leader of the New Democratic Party.[37] The Commission held public hearings and commissioned its own research, much of it based on analysis of the Nominal Roll of Uranium Miners.

The research clearly established, on a statistical basis, that lung cancer occurs much more frequently among uranium miners than would be expected in a comparable population of persons not exposed to more than the normal ionizing radiation.[38] The Commission condemned the self-regulatory model of regulation which had been created, or at least benignly encouraged, by the jurisdictional accommodations between federal and provincial regulatory authorities.[39] It criticized the failure both to inform and to involve labour unions in what it called the regulatory "responsibility system."[40] It concluded that "the technical means are available for meeting current standards at reasonable cost" and that "operations that do not comply should be closed."[41] Finally, it severely criticized regulatory authorities for their failure to conduct adequate research both with respect to compliance technology and with respect to monitoring and evaluating epidemiological data.[42]

(4) Intervention, Technology and Regulation

The uranium miners case is not an example of regulatory virtue. It illustrates that intervention in fact can flounder on a failure to ensure compliance. As Chapter 1 pointed out, the hidden world of day-to-day "administration" can simply be a new arena in which old battles and compromises are arranged. The important question is whether these arrangements and the resulting lack of regulatory virtue are intended or unintended. In this respect one must go beyond the stated intentions of policy makers. If behaviour over a sustained period of time is contrary to stated intentions one is entitled to believe that the resulting outcomes were due not to inertia or pragmatism, but that they were in large measure intended. Decisions to postpone action, or conscious decisions not to act, though more difficult to detect, are a major form of government intervention since they benefit some groups and classes and not others.

While acknowledging this important fact, it is important to stress that the rationales for such muted forms of intervention are often subtle and are effected by changing paradigms. One was certainly reflected in the closed, secretive model under which the AECB functioned. But this was reinforced by what can best be called a "weight of reliance" paradigm adopted by regulators.

The existing regulatory philosophy has been dominated by a paradigm which places the primary reliance on the regulated industry or firm for developing and presenting to the regulatory authorities their plans and designs for ensuring health, safety and security in their construction programs and operating activities. That such a general reliance is necessary seems a reasonable proposition. That the <u>degree or weight</u> of such reliance and dependence by regulatory authorities can become excessive and contrary to the public interest is, however, a point of legitimate dispute. The uranium miners case shows that the <u>degree</u> of dependence on industry plans and actions by both federal and provincial regulators is excessive. This tendency to depend excessively on the industry is worsened by the general practice of the regulators to subsume controls and standards <u>within</u> particular <u>individual licenses</u> rather than to engage in more general regulation-making. Thus, to a certain extent, each license becomes a unique "negotiated" deal between regulators and the firm.

Regulators point out that each mine is unique and that the adequacy of a company's proposals and designs become a matter of "experience" and "judgement" by regulators. Under these conditions regulatory authorities undoubtedly do coax and persuade (and perhaps threaten with sanctions) regulated firms to practice better health, safety and security practices. They undoubtedly learn from previous regulatory inadequacies. But it is difficult, if not impossible, for others not a direct party to the negotiated licensing processes to know if the license has indeed incorporated the best available technology or work practices available or that "lowest practicable exposures" are <u>in fact</u> being secured. (This is not to say that a more open, general rule-making approach will obtain this result either.)

Health standards for uranium miners have been made more stringent, but the degree of compliance has still not been such as to regularly meet those standards. Improvement has occurred only after much painful neglect and only through agonizingly slow regulatory processes. The explanation of the slowness and inadequacy of the regulatory process with respect to uranium miners undoubtedly rests primarily with political and economic variables. However, the specific role of science and technology in the nuclear regulatory process deserves understanding in its own right. The several aspects of the role of science and technology are ultimately related to both the nuclear status quo of the 1960s and to the joint governmental-industrial economic interest both in uranium sales and in the high stakes created by the emerging technical success of CANDU. However, each of the aspects identified in Chapter 3 (hypotheticality, the openness of regulatory processes, the relationship between causal knowledge and perceptions of political evidence, and deference to international standard setting bodies) remain an important part of the day-to-day regulatory process and hence become and area where reform and improved performance can occur. Several observations arise from the foregoing analysis of the uranium miners case.

First, in the specific realm of the health and safety of uranium miners, the concept of hypotheticality does not apply in the way that it may well apply at the middle or back end of the nuclear fuel cycle. The consequences of a failure to act are real: statistical, if not causal, knowledge exists, as to the health consequences of radiation exposure on uranium workers. The neglect of uranium mining health and safety, in comparison with other elements of nuclear safety (such as reactors, and medical uses), has been influenced by a nuclear regulatory climate which, in many respects, has retained the trappings of hypotheticality. This has been part of the process at least in so far as scientific attitudes toward, and pride in, the overall safety record of the general nuclear power program helped create a view in which the residual risk borne by uranium miners became something that could be easily ignored as a minor irritant in an otherwise commendable safety effort.

The processes through which a few "cases" of cancer among uranium miners, brought to the attention of regulators through compensation claims or specific political criticism, are transformed into statistical, and ultimately, causal knowledge are obviously difficult and complicated. Full causal links have not been established. Strong statistical knowledge was in evidence, however, as early as 1967 in the case of American studies, and in 1969 in preliminary Ontario data. The question then is how soon and how quickly regulators and their scientific advisors respond to such information. The burden of the analysis in this chapter strongly suggests that the response was extremely slow both with reference to the use made of foreign studies and with reference to positively encouraging the development of Canadian analysis. There was a failure to act expeditiously. A less charitable interpretation is that there was a conscious policy to ignore the redistributive consequences of both regulatory behaviour and research priorities on a particular economic group or class. The excesses of scientific caution shown in the processes of handling causal knowledge and evidence, when combined with the regulator's split personality of being both regulator and promoter and "manager" of the nuclear and uranium industries gave only the most intermittent attention to uranium workers.

There is little doubt that the Canadian nuclear regulatory process, until very recently, has been basically closed, with the involvement of the uranium workers being virtually non-existent. This has been evident in the derivation of standards, in monitoring and in day-to-day compliance. The extraordinary leverage and openness of the Ham Commission in Ontario has fortunately led to some very recent reforms. The Commission's recommendation to integrate the "responsibility system" has been adopted by the Ontario government. Henceforth regulatory responsibility will be centred in the Ministry of Labour rather than, as in the past dispersed among the Health and Mines ministries. Legal requirements to inform labour unions have been instituted. At the federal level, the AECB has begun to pay much more attention, both in its research and in its compliance practices, to the health of uranium miners. It has, however, been reluctant to seek out direct labour representation either on its committees or on the Board itself. It will also experience difficulties in finding independent, non-industry centres to which it can contract its applied occupationally related research.

Despite recent reforms, there are numerous lingering doubts about how long the reform processes will last. An immense effort was required to produce the recent changes. Most of the criticism came from outside the main circle of regulatory actors. Experience indicates that continuing reform is unlikely without a free and open exchange of knowledge and without the persistent criticism by organized interests such as the uranium miners. Without changes in science and technology priorities, in the development of scientific personnel, and indeed in the professional attitude of the nuclear regulatory community, the uranium miners are likely to continue to bear a grossly disproportionate share of the far from hypothetical human costs of Canada's nuclear program.

NOTES: Chapter 7

1. Royal Commission on the Health and Safety of Workers in Mines in Ontario, Report, (Toronto: Ontario Queen's Printer, 1977), pp. 79- 80. Hereafter cited as Ham Commission, Report.

2. See Science Council of Canada, Policies and Poisons, (Ottawa: Minister of Supply and Services Canada, 1978).

3. Ham Commission, Report, op. cit., pp. 33-35.

4. Ham Commission, Transcript of Hearings, January 16, 1975, p. 630.

5. Ibid., pp. 630-621.

6. Ham Commission, Report, op. cit., pp. 33-34.

7. Interviews by the author. See United Steel Workers of America, Brief to the Ham Commission (Toronto, June 1975).

8. G. Bruce Doern, The Atomic Energy Control Board (Ottawa: Law Reform Commission of Canada, 1977), pp. 62-65.

9. Ham Commission, Transcript of Hearings, May 27, 1975, pp. 4251-4252.

10. Ibid., January 16, 1975, pp. 636-654.

11. Text of Submission by Stephen Lewis, Ontario NDP Leader to Ham Commission (Toronto, February 18, 1975), pp. 5-6.

12. J.H.F. Jennikens, "The Role of Advisory Committees in the Licensing of Nuclear Facilities in Canada." Paper presented to IAEA, Athens, Greece, December 1974.

13. See Doern, op. cit., pp. 36-50.

14. Ibid., pp. 60-68.

15. For a case study of these evolving relationships in the 1960s see G. Bruce Doern, Science and Politics in Canada (Montreal: McGill-Queen's University Press, 1972), Chapter 4.

16. See Economic Council of Canada, Responsible Regulation (Ottawa: Minister of Supply and Services Canada, 1979), Chapter 5; and Hudson Janisch, "Policy Making in Regulation: Towards a New Definition of the Status of Independent Agencies in Canada," Osgoode Hall Law Journal, Vol. 17, No. 1, 1979, pp. 46- 106.

- 149 -

17. See *Canada Gazette*, Part 2, Vol. 108, No. 12, June 26, 1974.

18. See Science Secretariat, *Physics in Canada: Survey and Outline* (Ottawa: Queen's Printer, May 1967, pp. 228-233.

19. On the early politics and government-industry partnership, see H.V. Nelles, *The Politics of Development* (Toronto: Macmillan of Canada, 1974). Consolidation of occpuational health and safety regulation in Ontario was undertaken in the new *Occupational Health and Safety Act 1978*.

20. Ham Commission, *Hearings*, p. 5118.

21. *Ibid.*, p. 5128-5129.

22. *Ibid.*, p. 5500.

23. Ham Commission, *Report, op. cit.*, p. 5.

24. *Ibid.*, p. 77.

25. *Ibid.*

26. *Ibid.*, pp. 79-80.

27. *Ibid.*, pp. 88-89.

28. AECB, *Brief to Ham Commission* (Ottawa: June 1975).

29. A working level (WL) is a special measure of external radiation based on any combination of short-lived radon daughters in equilibrium with radon in one litre of air, which will result in the ultimate emission of 1.3×10^5 million electron volts (MeV); equivalent to one hundred picocuries per litre.

30. Federal Radiation Council, *Guidance for the Control of Radiation Hazards in Uranium Mining* (Washington, D.C.: FRC Report No. 8, Revised 1967).

31. Text of Submission by Stephen Lewis, op. cit., pp. 13-14.

32. J. Muller and W.C. Wheeler, "Causes of Death in Ontario Uranium Miners," Proceedings of the International Symposium on Radiation Protection in Mining and Milling of Uranium and Thorium (Bordeaux, France, September 9-11, 1974).

33. Ham Commission, Report, p. 77. See also text by Lewis, op. cit., pp. 15-17.

34. AECB, Brief to Ham Commission, op. cit.

35. Ibid.

36. Ibid.

37. See especially, Standing Committee on Supply. Natural Resource Estimates (Toronto: Ontario Legislature, May 21-23, 1974), pp. 840-920.

38. Ham Commission, Report, op. cit., p. 66.

39. Ibid., p. 6.

40. Ibid., p. 77.

41. Ibid., p. 97.

42. Ibid., p. 86.

Chapter 8

Intervention and Bargaining: The Ontario Hydro Long Term Uranium Contracts

Spurred by a desire to obtain a secure long term supply of uranium for its growing stable of nuclear reactors, the Government of Ontario authorized Ontario Hydro in February and March, 1978, to enter into long term contracts with Denison Mines and Preston Mines for the supply of uranium (U_3O_8). The combined contracts expire in 2020. The total value of the contracts is between $6 and $7 billion. The contracts are perhaps the longest term contractual arrangement ever entered into by a government in Canada with private enterprise. The magnitude and duration of the agreements, the use of the contract as an instrument, and the nature of the bargaining involved, make the Hydro uranium contracts a useful case study for an analysis of government intervention.[1]

The analysis of the decision process leading up to the signing of the contracts will proceed in four stages. We will first describe and summarize the main events in the contract decision process between 1972 and 1978. The second part of the chapter will examine the organizational characteristics of the decision process, particularly the relationships between Ontario Hydro and the Ontario Cabinet. This will be followed by an account of the contracts' main provisions, and finally by our preliminary assessment of the causes and consequences of government intervention through the contract device.

(1) <u>Main Events in the Contract Decision Process, 1972 to 1978</u>

(a) <u>The Search for Secure Supply</u>

In 1971 and 1972 George Gathercole, the Chairman of Ontario Hydro, and other senior Hydro officials became especially concerned about the need for a long term supply of uranium. The success of the Pickering reactors and the optimistic long range forecast of Hydro's growing electricity needs reinforced the long-recognized fact that uranium was the only relatively abundant and economic source of energy, coal reserves being virtually non-existent in Ontario. This concern about security of energy supply was paramount. Given Hydro's $14 billion capital investment in nuclear plants, both security of supply and price were important. By April 1977, it was estimated that Hydro would need 156 million pounds of uranium oxide to fuel its Douglas Point, Pickering 'A' and 'B', Bruce 'A' and 'B', and Darlington plants over 30 years at 80 percent load capacity.[2]

(b) Supply Alternatives and the Possibility of Acquisition

In 1973 Task Force Hydro, a special study group created a year earlier in response to criticism of lack of political control of Ontario Hydro, published its findings.[3] Of particular interest in this stage of our analysis was the Task Force suggestion that Hydro should proceed to acquire the uranium assets of Denison Mines, the holder of the largest low cost reserves then available. Denison had earlier (when uranium prices were in the doldrums) attempted to sell its Elliot Lake reserves without success. The purchase idea was given some further credence by the previous chairman of Hydro who wrote to the Minister of Energy suggesting the same course of action. Newly appointed to the new energy ministry, Darcey McKeough, while conceding that the possibility of acquiring its own mines should be considered, said he did not favour this route to obtain supply.[4]

To facilitate the supply objective Ontario Hydro retained D.S. Robertson and Associates to advise the corporation. In May 1974 the consultants outlined seven supply alternatives, namely:

1. fully negotiated long-term supply contracts;

2. negotiated contracts but with the federal government allocating a proportion of reserve to domestic customers and to impose some sort of control on the price payable by Canadian customers;

3. establishment of a Federal Uranium Marketing Board to purchase and resell all uranium produced in Canada and give Canadian customers a price preference;

4. stimulation of exploration by sale of uranium ore in ground to the federal government;

5. nationalization of the uranium industry by the federal government;

6. joint industry-Ontario government of Ontario Hydro exploration programs;

7. purchase of the shares or uranium assets of a uranium company.[5]

D.S. Robertson recommended to Ontario Hydro that the contract route (alternative 1) be the alternative pursued. Ontario Hydro, however, reiterated to the Minister of Energy on June 4, 1974, that,

> Acquisition of the Denison reserves is the key to Ontario Hydro' bargaining position now and in the future. In default of this it appears that price protection could only be attained through political pressure and/or legislative action.[6]

The Minister responded on June 14, 1974, that "I am convinced that there has to be a better way than simply buying a mine."[7]

After negotiations with Preston and Denison had commenced regarding a long term contract and there was no willingness of either firm to move from its position of demanding world prices for the uranium it sold to Ontario Hydro, a confidential study was commenced in February 1975, called Project Wellesley. The internal report presented to Ontario Hydro's Board of Directors recommended that it enter into negotiations to obtain a majority interest in Denison Mines through the purchase of shares. By the time the Project Wellesley report was presented, both Preston and Denison had shown a willingness to move from the previous position in which they demanded world prices for their uranium. As a consequence, Ontario Hydro did nothing with the recommendations. The Ontario Cabinet, in reviewing the progress that Hydro was making in its negotiations, reiterated its support for the contract option.

In the Robertson study little consideration was given to offshore supplies, mainly because Robertson felt that they could not get better than world price and, in addition, there existed the possibility that the supply might not be secure. At that time, it should be added, Australian supplies were not for export, South Africa had very little to offer because uranium there was a by-product of gold mining, and the U.S. had more reactors than available production.

Robertson got four responses: a small one from Gulf, a small one from Eldorado, and the Rio Algom (Preston) and Denison proposals. Thus the major constraint on Hydro's bargaining position with suppliers was clearly evident. Enough producers in 1974 did not exist for truly competitive offers. Only the Preston and Denison mines _together_ had enough to supply Hydro's needs. Hydro was not even able to play one off against the other.

Once the source of supply had been identified, Hydro still had the possibility of acquiring the supply in a number of ways. As Robertson pointed out, Hydro could buy the assets or shares of one or both of the mines. It could sign short term contracts. Hydro could enter into some kind of production-sharing agreement with the producers. It could try to get the federal government to nationalize one or both mines and then sell or otherwise divest itself of the holdings in Hydro's favour, or Hydro could try to get Ottawa to institute a two-price system for uranium.

However, several of the above possibilities were eliminated by the political philosophy of the Davis government expressed through Darcey McKeough. As we have seen, as early as 1973, it was made clear to Hydro that acquisition of a mine was not in accordance with the philosophy of the government. Throughout the negotiations with the producers, the actions of Hydro clearly indicate that this constraint was taken seriously.

Some evidence suggests that Project Wellesley was used to break the price deadlock. The price break in negotiations came in July 1975. The Project Wellesley report went to the Hydro board in August 1975. Although the study was supposed to be secret, news of it did circulate among the producers and they subsequently reconsidered the price question.

(c) <u>Federal Uranium Supply Policy and Bargaining Leverage</u>

It is useful to recall at this stage the existence of the federal uranium supply policy enunciated in September 1974 and noted briefly in Chapter 5.[8] The purpose of the policy was to protect the uranium supply needs of the domestic nuclear program of which Ontario Hydro was the key. The federal policy required producers to have sufficient uranium reserves to allow each nuclear power reactor, operating or planned for operation in 10 years into the future, to operate at an average of 80 percent capacity for 30 years from the start of the period, or for planned reactors, 30 years from the date they became operational.

Each mining company was to have a reserve margin allocated to it based on the ratio of its uranium resources to the total Canadian recoverable resources. The total recoverable Canadian resources are estimated by the federal government and include all ore that can be recovered at prices of up to twice the current world market price.

Domestic utilities were required to maintain a contract with producers which would ensure that each operating reactor, or committed reactor, could operate at an annual capacity of 80 percent for 15 years. For committed reactors not yet operating, the contract was to allow them to operate for 15 years from the date of their coming into service.

Contracts to export uranium were limited to a maximum of 10 years with contingent approval for an additional five years. The five year extension would be approved provided that no domestic utility required the uranium identified for export. The federal government also announced that it would use the stockpile of 13,000 tons of uranium that it had accumulated between the years 1963 to 1974 to cover shortages that might exist in the domestic market.

Ontario Hydro and the Government of Ontario felt that the federal policies required them to have long-term contracts for uranium supplies with producers, but that they gave them no leverage in negotiating favourable contracts in terms of price. This assessment was based upon the federal guidelines requiring that producers have a reserve amount of uranium ore available in the ground for the domestic market. In theory this could be kept indefinitely in the ground unprocessed. The federal policy does not require a specific proportion of the production to be allocated to the domestic market. Therefore, the producers could, in theory, export their total production, so long as they retained the necessary ore reserve in the ground. Also, producers, who were close (five years) to the exhaustion of their ore body, can apply for exemption from the reserve requirement if they can demonstrate that they had been unable to sign a contract with a domestic user for the reserve. Therefore, producers could potentially sell all their production, excluding the reserve, to export markets and then ask for exemption from the reserve requirements which would allow for their production to be totally dedicated to foreign utilities. There is, however, considerable doubt that the federal government would permit this situation to develop.

The federal policy did not provide for a two-price system, i.e., one price for the domestic market and one for the foreign market. While there were representations from the Ontario government to the federal government for a two-price system, the federal position did not change.[9] Indeed the federal Minister of Energy, Mines and Resources, Alastair Gillespie, stated in a letter to the Ontario Minister of Energy on November 4, 1977;

> With regard to the domestic market itself, our policy has always been to leave prices entirely to producers - consumer negotiations and I can see no situation that would change this.[10]

This federal policy is consistent with its thinking on the price of other fuels, where the domestic price of fuel is being raised, albeit slowly, to or near international levels.

Dr. O.J.C. Runnals, the Senior Advisor, Uranium and Nuclear Energy, with the federal Department of Energy, Mines and Resources, stated before the Ontario Select Committee on Hydro that the prices per pound of uranium contained in the two contracts signed by Hydro vindicated the federal policies. He felt that the contracts showed that domestic consumers could get an advantageous price without a two-price system.[11]

(d) <u>Renegotiation and Broader Energy Trade-Offs</u>

By mid-December 1975 Hydro had accepted in principle the Denison offer which it subsequently submitted to the Minister of Energy for approval. Such approval was necessary for two reasons. First, the <u>Power Corporation Act</u>, under which Hydro functions, ordinarily confers blanket authority on Hydro to secure fuel for any single approved plant.[12] Since the proposed contracts were not earmarked for any one plant, Cabinet approval was required. Second, regardless of the legal niceties, Hydro was simply unprepared "to go it alone" with this decision without the visible support of the Davis Cabinet. The sheer size of the contracts no doubt were important in this regard.

Between December 1975 and December 1977 the contracts were reviewed by officials of the Energy and Treasury departments and renegotiation of contract provisions took place. Late in 1977, frustrated by the lengthy delays, Denison through its principal owner Stephen Roman, gave Premier William Davis, with whom Roman enjoyed some political friendship, a three month deadline until February 28, 1978 to approve the contracts. Roman indicated that if there was no agreement he would sell uranium to other waiting foreign customers at the world price. While not enamoured at being driven to the bargaining wall by the eccentric and sometimes unpredictable Mr. Roman, senior Ontario officials essentially felt compelled to recognize two realities. Roman did have the uranium they needed at a lower-than-world price and he did have other customers to whom he could sell at least some of it at the world price.

It is important to recognize that while the contract negotiations were proceeding in 1976 and 1977 the Ontario government did attempt to secure federal assistance and leverage over the uranium producers. Ontario was not in a position to press this claim too hard, however, despite the fact that there was considerable federal animosity toward Roman because of earlier disputes with the Trudeau and Pearson governments over foreign sales to France in 1965 and foreign ownership in 1970.[13] Ontario's reluctance arose out of the larger bargaining and political needs in energy and constitutional matters. Increasingly in the 1970s, in the face of the resource power of Alberta and Saskatchewan, Ontario found itself more aligned with the federal government because both Ontario and the federal government had to balance consumer and producer interests in energy matters. In the nuclear field, moreover, Ontario was engaged in negotiations with the federal government over heavy water facilities and waste management.[14]

(e) The Select Committee Review: Obtaining Legitimacy

The final phase of the public decision process came on December 19, 1977, when Premier William Davis, anxious to secure a wider base of legitimacy and support for the contract, especially at a time of minority government, asked the recently appointed Ontario Legislature's Select Committee on Ontario Hydro chaired by a former leader of the provincial New Democratic Party, Donald C. MacDonald, and with a majority of opposition members on it, to investigate and approve the contracts. The committee had to report before the February 28th Denison deadline.

Chairman MacDonald expressed his hope that the Committee's recommendations might be adopted by the Government as their earlier recommendations on rate increases had been. Although it did remarkably well under the circumstances, Davis' expectation that the Committee would break down along party lines quickly materialized. This is evident on reading transcripts of committee meetings. George Ash and John Williams, both Tory members, continually underlined testimony favourable to the contracts, while Robert Nixon, the former Liberal leader, pressed for more detailed financial information, especially on possible excess profits. Evelyn Gigantes (NDP) tried to extract reasons for the rejection of the Project Wellesley report. On the final recommendations the Committee split along party lines with the Conservatives favouring the contracts while the Liberals and New Democrats deciding the contracts were not in the public interest. The Liberals were not willing to go as far as the NDP in suggesting that the assets of the uranium mines should have been acquired.[15]

The Committee had very severe constraints placed upon it about which it could do nothing other than to have rejected the assignment. These constraints, in addition to the already evident one of time, included a paucity of independent information. When the Committee was assigned the task of looking at the contracts, the documents had already been deemed acceptable by two sets of consultants. Both Hydro and the Ministry were represented by independent consultants from the resource, legal, and financial fields. Furthermore, Hydro staff, the Hydro board, the Ministry of Energy and the Premier had all agreed that these contracts were in the best interests of the people of Ontario.

The information the Committee received came overwhelmingly from these sources. Some independent market research studies such as one by McLeod, Young and Weir were available, but such sources were few. The Committee managed to hire some consultants, but they did not have much time to prepare in-depth analyses and consequently were only able to list some alternatives that had not been looked at. This in no way approached the detailed and exhaustive studies that had been done by David S. Robertson on behalf of Ontario Hydro, or the S.M. Stoller Corporation on behalf of the Ministry.

(f) Supply, Demand and Uncertainty

Although the Committee suffered from these informational and time inadequacies, there is one sense in which its experience was similar to that of the Government and Hydro in the earlier decision stages: uncertainty over future uranium supply and demand projections. The Committee was subjected to a variety of projections in a brief period of time. However, it is to be remembered that the Government and Hydro were subjected to an equal range, but over a much longer time period dating back to 1972. The contracts are fundamentally exercises in gauging and reducing uncertainty and shifting risks about the long term future. A brief review of these forecasts is therefore instructive in examining the causes and forms of intervention.[16]

The contracts will ultimately be judged by the future world price of uranium. This price will be affected by the demand for uranium in the next 40 years and also by the amount producers make available. The estimates of what will be available and how much demand there will be, as we have seen in Chapter 2, are very nebulous. This became quickly evident to the Committee when it tried to compare the estimates of future demand and supply presented by the various consultants and experts.

On the Ontario demand side, for example, a possible surplus of 65 million pounds could occur. As Figure 8.1 shows, the Denison and Preston contract would yield 198 million pounds. Hydro would need 156 million pounds of U_3O_8 to cover its basic projected fuel needs. This total assumed no more reactors after Darlington and a thirty year life cycle for current and committed reactors. Existing contracts cover 13 million pounds to meet needs to 1980 and part of the requirements through 1985. There is a possible need for an additional 10 million pounds to cover shortfalls between 1981-1993.

Figure 8.1

Possible Uranium Demand Scenario Resulting in Surplus

	Amounts Under Denison and Preston Contracts		198 million pounds
	Basic Need	156 million pounds	
Less:			
	Current Contracts	13 million pounds	143 million pounds
	MINIMUM EXCESS		55 million pounds
Plus:			
	Possible Additional Contracts in 1980s		10 million pounds
	MAXIMUM EXCESS		65 million pounds

Assumptions: 1. No More Reactors.
2. Current and Committed Reactors have only a 30 year life.

Source: Adapted from Ontario Select Committee on Ontario Hydro, Report on Proposed Uranium Contracts (Toronto: Ontario Queen's Printer, March 1978), p. 92.

Predictions of Western World demand vary depending on the expert. David S. Robertson and Associates, consultants to Hydro, indicated what happened to predictions made of installed nuclear capacity in 1970 as compared to predictions made in 1977. In 1970 it was estimated that the installed nuclear capacity in 1985 would approximate 650 GWe.[17] This prediction was lowered in 1977 to 330 GWe installed by 1985. Another estimate of nuclear capacity make in 1977 and used by McLeod, Young and Weir shows nuclear capacity in 1985 will be 278 GWe. Nuclear reactor orders in the U.S. also point to this decrease in demand for nuclear power. In 1972, 36 reactors were ordered. The figures for subsequent years are: 1973...46; 1974...22; 1975...5; 1976...3; 1977est...1; 1978est...0. These and other estimates clearly show that forecasts made in the early 1970s have had to be revised downward. In addition, electricity load forecasts by Hydro and other utilities of the growth anticipated in the early 1970s has not been as great as expected.[18]

The problems of estimating supply are even more difficult than of estimating demand. Robertson felt that supply will be tight during the life of the Hydro contracts. John Hogerton, representing the S.M. Stoller Corporation, energy consultants for the Ontario Ministry of Energy, did not think the situation would be as tight as Robertson, but agreed that the bottom line is the same. In his opinion: a high value should be placed, in today's uranium supply circumstances, on securing access to established reserves. It is in the individual utility's interest to cover its forward requirements for as long a term as is feasible from a contracting standpoint. The factors that S.M. Stoller Corp. believed would retard downward price movement for other than spot transactions, include:

- an important quotient of "irreversability" in the price rise that has taken place owing to the concomitant shift to higher cost ground;

- the fact that many producers, having by now done a substantial volume of "price in effect" contracting, have a vested interest in market price futures;

- in the case of certain countries with major uranium supply potential, the terms of export contracts are subject to government approval and the governments involved can be expected to try to support the level of pricing of a depletable energy resource; and

- most utilities have substantial uncovered requirements in and beyond the early 1980s and could not, even if they were so disposed, long defer procurement action.

S.M. Stoller concluded that, in the long run, the cost of production and exploration will follow a rising curve and the price trend in dollars would be upward.

The Committee was presented with an array of supply outlooks, ranging from Robertson's scenario of greatest scarcity in which prices would reach $100/pound, to the middle position of S.M. Stoller Corp. as outlined above, to predictions by Moss and Ball of prices dropping to $20/pound. The uncertainty of what will be the market price of uranium 30 or 40 years in the future makes a decision which must be made today very difficult. Those involved in this decision had to consider the scenario with the highest probability of occuring but they also had to examine those most in keeping with their risk-taking propensity. They had to hedge their bets but they had to bet. Hydro felt that there would be short supply until the turn of the century and thus decided to undertake long term contracts.

There are other elements of the decision process, including that of estimates of the amount of profit accruing to the producers, and the employment effects for uranium miners and uranium communities but we will leave these to our later description and analysis of the contracts themselves in section 3 below. In the meantime, it is important to develop an appreciation of the evolving developments in policy machinery, especially in the relations between Ontario Hydro and the Ontario Cabinet.

(2) Ontario Hydro and the Ontario Cabinet: Control, Independence and Intervention

Ontario Hydro was created as a publicly-owned electrical utility because of enormous business pressure in the early part of this century against "gouging" on electricity rates by private utilities. It was to be an instrument to secure cheap abundant power to fuel the industrial development of Ontario.[19] Though owned by a government, it was intended to be independent of partisan day-to-day politics. It became both independent and powerful. An organization of internationally-respected engineering, technical and financial experts, it, like AECL, has enormous collective pride in its achievements. No Crown corporation is, of course, ever totally independent of the government, but Hydro more than most, protected by successive Chairmen and board members with a judicious mixture of political and business acumen, had managed to secure great independence through much of the heady expansionist years of the 1940s, 1950s and 1960s. In the 1970s, however, like so many other public sector institutions, it has had to develop new responses including a highly selective concept of independence in the face of persistent public criticism and a rapidly changing energy, social and economic environment.

(a) The Main Dimensions of Interdependence

There are three important dimensions of the relationship between Hydro and the Ontario Cabinet. These include legal relationships, accepted conventions, and practices, and public political perceptions of the relationship. The legal basis of the relationship resides primarily in the Power Corporation Act (RSO 1970, Chapter 354 as amended) although several other statutes including the Public Utilities Act are also important.[20] There are at least 25 areas in the Power Corporation Act where Hydro must obtain permission of the Government before it can act. There is agreement between Hydro and the government that Hydro is not legally obliged to take other policy directives from the government. Indeed, Hydro board members have on occasion expressed the view that the Board might be derelict in their duty under the Power Corporation Act if it did.

Further legal ambivalence arises out of the fact that the Ministry of Energy Act, which created the new energy ministry in 1973, assigns the Minister of Energy responsibility for the Power Corporation Act. The Power Corporation Act, however, can and has led to the interpretation that the Hydro Board of Directors is accountable, not to the Minister, but through him to the Legislative Assembly of Ontario. This statutory ambivalence is of considerable import and often politically convenient for both parties. For example, it effects the kinds of contact and consultations which the Minister and his deputy can have with, and expect from, Hydro. The Deputy Minister's role is especially difficult since he must advise his Minister but may now know of Hydro's latest decisions. Hydro officials hold fast to the view that they are not legally linked to the Deputy Minister of Energy. Yet, the energy ministry was created to achieve better political control of energy policy in general and Hydro in particular. The need for such control had been pointed out in political criticism for years and acknowledged by Task Force Hydro when it reported in 1973. The first Minister of Energy, Darcey McKeough, set out to exercise such control but he and subsequent ministers have been caught in the inevitable grey zone between control and independence.

Conventions certainly exist that Hydro must be sensitive to the Government's wishes and difficulties and that the latter should not attempt to exercise detailed control. It follows, therefore, that there should be advance consultation and warnings of potential dangers, but how early in the process and at what level of detail is always a genuine source of both uncertainty and dispute. Despite efforts to develop written guidelines to clarify relationships, both parties know that the task is virtually impossible, and concede, moreover that there is often mutual advantage in the ambiguity.

What exists, therefore, is what one person interviewed calls an "umbrella theory of independence and control." If on any particular decision the situation is perceived to be politically sunny then the independence of Hydro is not a matter is dispute. If things are cloudy then both seek the umbrella of ambiguity. This is not entirely a workable metaphor, however, since it presumes that both parties characterize the political weather the same way. Moreover, where decisions such as the Hydro uranium contracts evolve over several years, the situation can be affected not only by changes in (short term) political weather but also by changes in (long term) political climate.

It should not be surprising that broader public perceptions of the Hydro-Government relationship should be equally ambivalent. Hydro is in one sense a kind of symbol of almost forty years of Tory rule, and of smug, confident economic development. There is also genuine concern that Hydro makes energy policy and that it should not. There was concern about Hydro expansion plans, a prime factor in the decision to establish the Porter Royal Commission on Electric Power Planning. That Hydro has enormous political and economic power is not in serious doubt, but its relationship with government, as the uranium contracts case study shows, is not straightforward or simple and hence illustrates the problems of political intervention by Cabinet through an enterprise of the state.

(b) <u>Intra-Cabinet Decision Routes</u>

It is also necessary to appreciate that the routes through which Hydro-related decisions travel <u>within</u> the Ontario Cabinet policy and decision system are numerous. There are few one-way streets and many blind alleys. The decision route depends on the issue and its strategic political importance. For example, increasingly in the 1970s, but especially beginning in 1975, political leverage over Ontario Hydro began to be exercised by the Ministry of Treasury and Economics. This arose out of growing skepticism of Hydro's enormous market demands for capital based on what both Treasury and Energy ministry officials felt were highly questionable and costly load factor estimates, including very high reserve excess capacity. This coincided with a new energy consciousness induced by OPEC's oil price hikes as well as by federal and provincial concern about the need to both control and coordinate public borrowings abroad. Concerns such as these eventually found their way into numerous cabinet committees and ministerial discussions. In this instance at least, and over a fairly long period of time, Hydro proposals were received by an alliance with a somewhat different though not totally opposed view of the world.

In the case of the development of Ontario's view of Bill C-14, the federal Nuclear Control and Administration Act, for example, the decision was essentially hammered out in the Cabinet Committee on Resources and Development, and later communicated to the federal-provincial Mines Ministers meeting on this subject. In contrast to the above example, the uranium contracts decision travelled a somewhat narrower route, in this case largely one involving only the Premier's Office, the Energy Ministry and Hydro with the Cabinet being brought in at a final stage following the review of the contracts by the Select Committee.

Of necessity, the above discussion of the evolving relationship between Hydro and the Ontario cabinet and government has been brief and incomplete. It cannot possibly capture other nuances and relationships which exist in the wider context of governing in a large, industrialized province in a federal system of government. At the same time, however, the uranium contracts case and government intervention cannot be fully understood except in the context of these relationships.

(3) The Denison and Preston Contracts

Appendices B and C summarize the main elements of the Denison and Preston contracts respectively. The two contracts were negotiated separately and contain different provisions. They cover a forty year period, are worth between $6 and 7 billion and will supply 198 million pounds of uranium.[21]

(a) <u>Major Provisions</u>

The Denison contract stipulates that Denison is to dedicate its uncommitted uranium reserves at Elliot Lake to supplying Ontario Hydro. Denison is also to dedicate, in part, its existing mine, plant, and supporting facilities to the project from 1980 to 1993 and in total for the remainder of the agreement to the year 2001. Denison is to commit its management and know-how to the expansion of its existing mine, plant, and supporting facilities and to subsequent operations.

Ontario Hydro undertakes to purchase 126 million pounds of uranium concentrate on an agreed schedule between 1980 and 2001, subject to certain provisions covering the price competitiveness of the uranium and Ontario Hydro's ability to use it. The price paid will be equal to a negotiated base price plus one-half the difference to the market (world) price. Hydro advances to Denison between 1978 and 1984 the cost of the expansion of Denison's existing facilities, estimated at $151 million (1975 dollars), including an initial advance of $25 million. These advances are to be repaid to Ontario Hydro without interest, as credit against uranium delivered. In terms of 1976 dollars, the Denison contract is worth about $4.1 billion (undiscounted).

The Rio Algom/Preston contract calls for Preston to carry out an engineering study up to a limit of $1.5 million. Preston dedicates the entire Stanleigh ore body of an estimated 72 million pounds of uranium oxide to Ontario Hydro. Preston is to construct the necessary facilities, with Rio Algom managing the construction and the subsequent operation on behalf of Preston. Ontario Hydro agrees to purchase from Preston some 2 million pounds/year starting in 1983 and is to continue to do so (subject to termination provisions) until the reserve is exhausted. Also, at Ontario Hydro's option, the production rate may be increased to 4 million pounds/year starting any time between 1988 and 1994. The price paid by Hydro will be the higher of a negotiated base price or base plus one-third the difference to the world price. Ontario

Hydro will advance the funds needed to construct the mining and milling and supporting facilities, estimated at $188 million (1975 dollars), for the basic project and an additional $140 million if Hydro opts to expand to the higher production level after 1988. These advances are to be repaid without interest by credits against uranium delivered. In terms of 1976 dollars, the Preston contract is worth $2.4 billion (undiscounted).

(b) <u>Profit to the Producers</u>

The most controversial aspect of the contracts, and the one which received most media attention, was the question of the amount of profit the two producers would make as a result of these contracts. Both contracts call for a $5.00/pound (escalated) profit to be included in the base price.[22] This represents a profit with apparently little risk involved and was the source of major controversy in the Select Committee. In addition to this $5.00 figure, Denison stands to add one-half the difference between base and world prices while for Preston the added profit would be one-third the difference to the world price (if the latter exceeds the base price). Estimating the profits to Denison, the Stoller Corp. took the world price to be $41.00, the base price to be $26.00, which gives a profit of $12.50/ lb. or approximately $1.5 billion for the contracted 126 million pounds. The cost to Hydro at $33.50/pound would be $4.2 billion (in 1976 dollars). For Preston the profit would amount to $628 million while cost to Hydro would be $2.4 billion. If the producers were able to sell these quantities at the projected world price, the profit to Denison would be $2.5 billion while that accruing to Preston would be $1.1 billion.

John F. Utley, representing Deloitte, Haskins and Sells, the financial consultants for the Ministry of Energy, tried to lessen the Committee's distaste for the $5.00/pound profit figure. He pointed out that reserves in the ground in some places in the U.S. were being sold at prices from $5.00 - $7.00 U.S. and that these mining companies did not have nearly the expertise of Denison or Preston.[23] Also, there is a management fee cost of 10 to 15 percent of production costs in the American contracts. Thus assuming at $20 cost (conservative) this equals $2.00 to $3.00 U.S. He concluded that the purchase of reserves in the ground and management of the reserves is generally worth between $7 to $10 U.S. or $8 to $11 Canada. In his opinion the $5.00/pound fee was reasonable. What he did not take into account in this analysis was the value of the interest free advances to Denison and Preston (see (c) below).

S.M. Stoller Corp. told the Ministry that the pricing formula provides an incentive for producer-efficiency. Since the producer's total profit is a function of the differential between base and market prices, it is also a function of his "costs" (see Appendices B and C) which can be inflated! It is therefore not necessarily in the producers' interests to keep operating costs down so as to maximize profits if he finds the utility of inflated costs greater than that of additional profits. This does not answer the nagging question, in the case of Denison, of who gets the cheaper-to-mine high grade ore, the Japanese (with whom Denison has contracts) or Hydro. It should be noted here that federal supply policies do not specify the quality of ore to be supplied to Canadian users.

None of the submissions to the Committee seemed to dispel the unease some members felt about the producers getting such large relatively risk-free profits. The Committee counsel indicated that the government still would have three possible options it could use after the fact. It could institute a special tax, the assets could still be bought, or the government could still try to get Ottawa to install a two-price system for uranium. The decision to sign the contracts, in effect, foreclosed the second and third options. As for the first, the contracts provide for any future tax to be included in the base price and thus passed on to Hydro. Denison also managed to include a price protection clause in its contract that would force Hydro to increase its price to Denison if anyone else in the geographic area makes better profit than Denison. This was a clause which no one liked, but apparently Hydro could not get out of it, or did not try.

The question of whether or not the uranium cartel, which existed between 1972 and 1975 (see Chapter 1), helped push the world price of uranium to its present level was raised in the Select Committee's review. The consultants generally felt that the price was not affected, that indeed, the cartel price followed U.S. domestic prices. The Ministry's legal consultants, McMillan, Binch, assured the Committee that if the price paid by Hydro to Denison or Preston was affected by a cartel of which the producers were members, Hydro would have cause for action against the producers to recover the difference between the artificial cartel price and a fair and equitable price.[24] The wording in the Preston contract is quite clear - "fair and equitable free market price" - while that in the Denison contract omits mention of world price. It simply states "fair and equitable price."

(c) The Advances

The contracts provide for large advances to both producers. Denison is to receive sufficient funds from Hydro, interest free, for the expansion of its mining facilities from 10,000 tons of ore per day to 21,200 tons/day and for expansion of its milling facilties from 7,100 tons of ore/day to 15,000 tons. This expansion is to take place from 1976-1985 at an estimated capital cost of $151,260,000 in 1975 dollars (undiscounted).

The advances to Preston are to refurbish the existing Stanleigh facilties and construct additional facilities as necessary. When completed, capacity will permit the mining and milling of uranium ore at an average of 5,000 tons of ore per milling day for not less than 340 milling days per year. In the long run this will amount to 2 million pounds of U O annually. This expansion is to take place from 1978 to 1985 at an estimated capital cost of $188.5 million (1975 dollars, undiscounted).

Preston will get funds for the engineering study and to design, construct and operate its Stanleigh project. The advances to Denison are for expansion. In both agreements advances are made monthly for costs expected or incurred with Hydro having strong rights of audit. Denison is to get $25 million immediately upon signing the contracts. There was a difference between the estimates of capital costs by Preston and Denison on the one hand and Robertson on the other. These were not alternative studies. Robertson looked at the Denison and Preston figures and came up with a number which was $88 million less. The two sets of figures probably represent the high and low estimates for such an endeavor, but it is here that Hydro will have to use its audit rights.

The advances to Denison, especially the $25 million, were also controversial because it was felt that these funds would help to meet Denison's commitments to the governments of Japan and Spain. Deliveries to Hydro do not begin until 1980 and the bulk of the deliveries do not come until 1994. Yet the contract does not provide for any recompense to Hydro should this money go to help fulfill other contracts, as it surely will.

It must be pointed out that if Denison had borrowed the money for capital expansion themselves, they would probably have paid more than Hydro, and this cost would have been built into the base price. Nonetheless, the interest-free advances left a bad taste in some Committee members' mouths. As Stuart Smith, the leader of the provincial Liberals, pointed out, to catch up with its Japanese contracts Denison needs to expand its capacity and to justify expansion on an economic scale, the company needs an additional long term sales contract.[25] Not only did they get the contract to justify expansion on an economic scale, they got the money to do the expansion as well.

(d) Control, Security and Flexibility

The contracts give Hydro strong rights of audit in the expansion of Denison as well as the right to participate in the decision making process of expansion. With Preston, data on expenditures which have already been incurred must be produced month to month against advances to Preston for refurbishing the Stanleigh property.

The Select Commitee was concerned that the advances to Denison might be used to increase capacity to fulfill other contracts. It was given no assurances that this would not happen. There is a possibility that Denison will draw on the high grade ore to fulfill Japanese contracts, leaving Hydro with lower grade ore - hence the greater recover costs can then be passed on to Hydro because they would be included in the base price.

Hydro has the right to terminate the Denison agreement under several circumstances: First, if before completion of expansion, a change occurs in the laws of Canada or Ontario, which would result in Hydro not being able to use its nuclear power generating facilities, then supplies can be terminated as of the end of the following year. In such a situation, Hydro would have to pay Denison's costs of continuing the expansion to the effective date of termination (if Denison decided to proceed with expansion) or bring expansion to an orderly termination. The portion of Hydro's advances to Denison not repaid or not payable on the effective dates of termination will be forfeited by Hydro. Second, if the base price exceeds the world price for five consecutive years, any time after 1985, Hydro may terminate the agreement as of the end of the following years. The cost to Hydro is the forfeiture of advance not repaid or repayable on the effective date of termination. Third, a force majeure provision operates for five years (on either party).[26]

The second provision means that the earliest that deliveries could be stopped, should base price exceed world price, would be 1991, leaving Hydro to pay higher than market price for more than eleven years. The Ministry of Energy's consultants viewed these termination provisions as beneficial to Hydro in light of three main factors: the security of supply achieved by Hydro; the fact that the expansion is being undertaken largely to meet Hydro requirements; and the benefits of a lower than world price.

Provisions in the Preston contract allow Hydro to terminate if the project study undertaken by Preston to determine the technical and economic feasibility of the rehabilitation and expansion of the Stanleigh mine reveals: a project cost estimate in excess of 10% over the original estimate of $188.5 million plus escalation; ore reserves less than 80 percent of the forecast 72 million pounds of U_3O_8; basic operating cost estimates more than 10 percent greater than the original estimate; or if the calculated production output averages less than 80 percent of the forecast 2 million pounds of U_3O_8 per year, or averages less than 1.9 million pounds/year for the total supply period. The cost to Hydro for such termination is the cost of the study ($1.5 million).

S.M. Stoller Corp. concluded that this is a highly desirable provision because it allows Hydro to confirm the economic desirability of the Preston offer before making a final commitment to the project. Once the development program has begun, Hydro can terminate if the then current capital cost estimate exceeds today's estimates, plus escalation, by 20 percent. This is to protect Hydro against large errors in estimates made during the engineering study as well as those in previous estimates. In such circumstances Hydro would forfeit all unreimbursed advance payments. Finally, Hydro may terminate the Preston contract at its convenience at any time on five years notice, with forfeiture of unreimbursed advance payments and payment of shutdown costs.

In the event of oversupply, Hydro has two options: to curtail supplies or to sell the excess. Hydro can reduce the volume provided for in the Denison contract in increments of five percent per year up to a maximum of 25 percent. The Preston contract allows Hydro to reduce commitments by up to 15 percent. Hydro can sell the uranium it does not require either through Denison as agent or, if Denison is unable to do so for a period of 18 months, by itself. The profits are split between the two parties. A similar provision exists with Preston, Hydro acting as agent if Preston is unable to sell within nine months.

Hydro's security is ensured through first mortgages on the two mining properties. The consultants have determined that Denison has good title to its assets and therefore they can be mortgaged. A first mortgage to Hydro with an initial limit of $250 million can be increased if advances go above $250 million. However, there is a provision for a prior encumbrance in favour of a third party, starting at $100 million up to a maximum of $300 million. Thus Hydro could wind up with what amounts to a second mortgage. There are no prior encumbrances in the Preston contract. In the event of default, Hydro could operate the mine.

(e) The Producers' Inducements to Bargain

All references to the quality of good corporate citizenship in Ontario to the contrary notwithstanding, the goals of the producers were clearly to secure as riskless a substantial profit as they could successfully extract from Hydro and from the Ontario government. Preston saw an opportunity to reclaim its Stanleigh mine with the help of interest-free loans of $151 million (1978 dollars) and to profit to the tune of $628 million over the life of the contract. Denison could look forward to an estimated $1.5 billion in profits, in the long run, and interest-free funds to expand its facilities to meet more immediate commitments. John Kostiuk, President of Denison Mines Limited, echoed the corporate citizenship motives suggested by Dr. John Runnals before the Select Committee:

> there is in all of us an innate feeling to try to help each other out in a community sense. I would have though that as good corporate citizens these companies are saying, look, we're going to be around here as corporations long after we as individuals have passed by.[27]

Other explanations related to profit and the reduction of uncertainty are ultimately more convincing.

At the time negotiations commenced, the uranium market was awakening from a decade of low prices. The uranium producers had experienced previously a boom to bust situation in the late 1950s and early 1960s. In 1973, it was obvious that the market was turning around.[28] While the long-term prospects of the uranium industry appeared favourable, there were factors that could cause the bright picture of the future to fade quickly. One such variable was greater government intervention. If the Canadian government moved to totally close export markets or severely restrict them, the favourable position that the producers found themselves in would be quickly eroded and the domestic user would begin to have a more advantageous position. In fact, during the course of negotiations with producers, the government of Ontario asked that a suspension be placed on export contracts. While the Canadian government rejected this proposal at the time, there was no guarantee that it would maintain the position in the future. In comparison to the other domestic users of uranium, Ontario Hydro is a giant. Therefore, if there were more severe controls on exports, and the mining companies did not have contracts with Ontario Hydro, their business prospects would be much less favourable.

There appears to be another reason why the companies were interested in reaching an agreement with Hydro. The amounts of uranium and time periods involved were so significant, and the guaranteed level of profitability so high (and tied directly to the world price), that if this business opportunity had been lost by either of the producers it might never have come along again.

One final reason for the signing of the contracts by the producers was the possibility, however remote, of a government effort to either purchase their shares or assets. While the producers in their testimony before the Select Committee denied that this was ever discussed, it would appear that they did know that Ontario Hydro was assessing this alternative.

(4) Intervention and Bargaining

With the advantage of hindsight, and depending upon how one ranks the several values at stake, it is easy to see how the contracts could lead to quite different evaluations of whether this particular instance of government intervention was in the "public interest" or has merely benefitted certain private interests. Ontario Hydro and the Conservative Government of Ontario could certainly argue from their perspective that the contracts served their view of the public interest because they:

- provide a guaranteed supply of uranium necessary to fuel the existing and committed nuclear reactors that Ontario Hydro possesses;

- allow Ontario Hydro to purchase its uranium fuel at less than the World market price;

- fully meet the federal government policies as they pertain to domestic utilities;

- in comparison with other uranium contracts, the terms of these contracts seem to be more favourable to Ontario Hydro; and

- utilize a domestic Ontario resource and secure stable and long term employment in a depressed region of the province.

Those with fundamentally different preferences for government intervention could easily and convincingly point to the failure to intervene through government acquisition of the mines. Such an opportunity was particularly attractive in the early 1970s when uranium prices were much lower. This option was foreclosed primarily because of the ideology of the government which opposed more public ownership, but also because there existed some considerable uncertainty as to the political (including electoral) and economic consequences of such a decision. Ideology did not prevent intervention, but it did influence the form and hence some of the consequences.

Intervention also required bargaining amidst great uncertainty. It involved bargaining about the bearing of risks (adverse outcomes) by all parties. It is important to stress, however, that foreclosing the acquisition option, even though it was later used as a lever in bargaining, essentially confined the nature of the bargaining to a narrower terrain. Bargaining in this terrain, however, involved two separate contracts. Accurately guessing what the other parties would do and could do was difficult. Some aspects of the bargains are questionable. These include:

- the clause in the Denison contract guaranteeing profitability in comparison to other Elliot Lake mining companies (therefore Denison gets $5.00/lb profit for sure plus more if its "opportunity costs" are higher);

- the failure to eliminate the exploration component ($.50/lb) of the base price in the Denison contract (since no additional exploration was required - the reserves were known);

- the failure to require higher production in the 1980s to meet Ontario Hydro anticipated uranium requirements;

- the failure to specify the quality of ore to be supplied in the early stages of the Denison contract (or to put a limit on operating costs); and

- the failure (in the light of previous inadequacies) to secure more specific contractual obligations regarding health and safety of miners.

The uranium contracts case shows, not unusually, that the government's interventionist strategy conferred great benefits on private interests. It is also a case which involved an apparent political leap of faith and embraced a time period which governments are not ordinarily accustomed to taking. It is important to stress, however, that there are some "fall back" provisions in the contracts. Hence, in the final analysis, a relatively heroic forty-year undertaking can be seen to be somewhat more incremental in nature than first surmised. The contracts were major undertakings however. Thus one is entitled to ask what would prompt the Ontario government, inclined, like all governments, to proceed gradually to take this political and economic plunge. The answer lies in part in the combined influence of three variables. These include the enormous size of the capital already invested in the Hydro nuclear installations; the relatively low proportion (in comparison with other fuels) that uranium fuel costs are to total reactor operating costs; and the emerging "paradigms" of economic management which increasingly stressed, in contrast to the earlier 1960s concern over Keynesian short term demand management, the <u>supply</u> side of the macro economic equation. The latter almost by definition required a longer term view. The supply paradigm was usefully joined in the late 1970s by renewed concern about <u>security</u> of energy supply and hence further induced a climate in which non-incremental decision leaps could be seriously contemplated and, occasionally, taken. The asking of the visceral question of "what will happen when the lights go out," is, in the final analysis, a relatively thoughtless one. However, in the short run psychology of political intervention, the value of the question to those who ask it is not to be underestimated.

NOTES: Chapter 8

1. The assistance of Peter Akers in the development of background information for this chapter is gratefully acknowledged. The analysis is based on the proceedings, transcripts and numerous background papers and exhibits of the Ontario Select Committee on Ontario Hydro as well as on numerous interviews with officials familiar with the transaction and involved in the nuclear policy process.

For a general discussion see Select Committee on Ontario Hydro, Report on Proposed Uranium Contracts (Toronto: Ontario Queen's Printer, March 1978).

2. Ontario Hydro Long Range Forecast, 48A April 1977.

3. See Task Force Hydro, Report Number Three: Nuclear Power in Ontario (Toronto: Ontario Queen's Printer, 1973); and Select Committee Investigating Hydro Ontario, First Report, A New Public Policy Direction for Ontario Hydro (Toronto: Ontario Queen's Printer, 1976).

4. See Minister of Energy, Statement to the Select Committee of the Legislature on Uranium Supply Alternatives. January 31, 1978.

5. Ibid., p. 15. See David S. Robertson and Associates, Report on Alternative Methods of Securing Uranium Supplies (Toronto: May 22, 1974).

6. Briefing Paper for Meeting on June 4, 1974, between the Chairman of Ontario Hydro, G.E. Gathercole and the Minister of Energy, W.D. McKeough.

7. Minister of Energy, W.D. McKeough. Letter dated June 14, 1977, to Chairman of Ontario Hydro, G.E. Gathercole.

8. Statement by the Honourable Donald S. Macdonald, Minister of Energy, Mines and Resources, on Canada's Uranium Policy, September 5, 1974.

9. Malcolm Rowan, "Nuclear Policy and Federal-Provincial Relations," in G. Bruce Doern and R.W. Morrison (eds.) Canadian Nuclear Policies (Montreal: Institute for Research on Public Policy, 1980) Chapter 14.

10. Quoted in Telex dated February 14, 1978, from Hon. Reuben Baetz, Minister of Energy to Hon. Alastair Gillespie, federal Minister of Energy, Mines and Resources.

11. See Select Committee on Ontario Hydro Affairs, Transcript of Hearings, February 1st, 1978.

12. Interviews.

13. See Department of Energy, Mines and Resources, A Brief Submitted to the Cluff Lake Board of Inquiry, Regina, Saskatchewan, April 1977. Appendix 6.

14. Rowan, op. cit.

15. Select Committee on Ontario Hydro, Report on Proposed Uranium Contracts (Toronto: Ontario Queen's Printer, 1978), pp. 131-144.

16. Ibid., pp. 94-97.

17. GWe is an abbreviation for "gigawatt electrical." One GWe is equal to one thousand megawatts electrical.

18. Royal Commission on Electrical Power Planning, A Race Against Time (Toronto: Ontario Queen's Printer, 1978) Chapter 2.

19. See H.V. Nelles, The Politics of Development (Toronto: Macmillan of Canada, 1974).

20. See Government of Ontario, The Power Corporation Act, Office Consolidation (Toronto: Ontario Queen's Printer, September 1975).

21. Select Committee on Ontario Hydro, op. cit.

22. Denison base price = operating costs + depreciation + mining tax + $5.00/lb. (escalated) + $.50/lb. (future exploration costs).

    Preston base price = operating costs + depreciation + mining tax + $5.00/lb. (escalated).

23. Select Committee on Ontario Hydro, Transcript of Hearings, January 18, 1978.

24. On this controversy see Select Committee on Ontario Hydro, <u>Report on Proposed Uranium Contracts</u>, op. cit., pp. 36-37.

25. <u>Ibid.</u>, p. 42.

26. McMillan, Binch, "Submission to Minister of Energy. Select Committee on Hydro Affairs," Exhibit 4.

27. Select Committee on Ontario Hydro Affairs, <u>Transcript of Hearings</u>, February 1st, 1978, p. H-16-30-2.

28. See Donald J. Lecraw, "Uranium Supply and Demand: Implications for Policy," in G. Bruce Doern and R.W. Morrison (eds.) <u>Canadian Nuclear Policies</u> (Montreal: Institute for Research on Public Policy, 1980) Chapter 5.

Chapter 9

Concluding Observations

The objective of this study has been to examine the role of government intervention in the Canadian nuclear industry. It was not intended to be a comprehensive analysis of all Canadian nuclear energy policies per se. While I have provided background material on the major elements of nuclear policy and on the evolution of the nuclear policy process, I have by no means done justice to many critical aspects of the nuclear debate, including long term waste management and reactor safety, proliferation of nuclear weapons, heavy water supply, foreign ownership, and federal involvement in the formation of an international uranium cartel in the early 1970s.

Against a general background of the politics, economics and organization of the nuclear policy field I have examined three "intervention" case studies in considerable detail. Together these case studies span the past three decades of Canada's nuclear history and deal with several phases of the nuclear fuel cycle. I have stressed that an historical understanding of intervention in any industry is essential, especially since in recent years there has been much simple sloganeering about government intervention.

While an examination of three case studies gives us some basis on which to judge the nature of intervention, it must be recognized that case studies by their very nature restrict one's ability to generalize, though not to learn and understand. In this concluding chapter I will first summarize the three cases in relation to the determinants of government intervention. I will then present some tentative general observations about intervention. In the final section I will offer conclusions about some major consequences of intervention in the nuclear industry, speculate on the likely patterns of intervention in nuclear policy in the 1980s and finally draw attention to weaknesses in nuclear policy, organization, and administration.

(1) The Three Case Studies: A Summary of Determinants

It should not be surprising to observe that the determinants of intervention are numerous and that it is usually difficult to assign precise weights to them. Furthermore, it is difficult to show particular connections between specific determinants and instruments of intervention. I discussed these determinants in Chapter 1 and referred to them again in the general background survey in Chapter 2 and 3. Here I will summarize the determinants in the more specific context of the three case studies examined in the three preceding chapters.

The determinants on which I focus are:

- Ideology - general beliefs about the proper role of government in relation to private and market activity, usually ranged along a conservative, liberal and socialist continuum.

- Objectives - the more specific purposes of public policy in the policy field in question and in closely related fields of public policy.

- Paradigms - reasonably coherent series of principles which express current assumptions about how to proceed in the narrower terrain of a policy field.

- Physical and Technological Realities - the spatial, technical and material characteristics of a given policy field or problem.

- Economic - the domestic and international allocative characteristics of the field but also including the distributional implications.

- Intergrovernmental Relations - the degree of federal-provincial and international conflict and/or cooperation.

- Interagency Relations - the degree of inter-agency conflict and/or cooperation within a single level of government.

The three cases are summarized under the above headings portrayed in Figure 9.1.

Ideology: The reactor program case study showed that at one point there was a strong ideological preference to have the private sector heavily involved in the program but that other factors intervened to prevent this from occuring. In the uranium miners case, ideological preferences for a self-regulatory mode of operation were present in Ontario. They were more muted at the federal level, but one can fairly conclude that the regulatory mode, as it affected uranium mining, was influenced by ideological preferences. The uranium contracts case also showed clearly that ideology helped foreclose the option of acquiring the uranium mines from their private owners.

Objectives and Paradigms: Ideologies and beliefs subtly interact with objectives and with paradigms. In the reactor program case, concern about security was initially predominant, but later a positive faith in technology, especially in the Sputnik era, was dominant. The willingness, in the 1950s, to engage in technical leapfrogging and in acts of technological faith present, however, a sharp contrast to the uranium miners case. There scientific norms induced supreme caution in interpreting claims regarding the casual link between hazards and the deaths of miners. In the latter case scientific norms served as a clear retardant to aggressive regulatory action.

There can be little doubt that some aspects of regulatory intervention were influenced by a desire to protect health and safety while ensuring employment. But trade-offs had to be made. Far more often than not, the health and safety of workers was <u>subordinated</u> to the economic interests of uranium mine owners and

Figure 9.1

THE THREE CASE STUDIES: SUMMARY OF DETERMINANTS OF INTERVENTION

DETERMINANTS	CASE 1: REACTOR PROGRAM	CASE 2: URANIUM MINERS	CASE 3: HYDRO CONTRACTS
1. Ideology (general views about the proper role of government)	- C.D. Howe's Strong preference for large private sector investment	- preference for self regulation	- McKeough and Davis preference for private ownership
2. Objectives	- security - faith in technology	- health and safety - employment - scientific caution about causual knowledge	- security of supply - price and profit - employment
3. Paradigms (assumptions about development within the policy field)	- atoms for peace	- reliance on mines for proposing safe work environment - worker as the problem versus work as the problem - closed regulatory process	- hard vs soft energy paradigms - greater concern for economic supply management
4. Physical and Technological Realities	- reactor alternatives in other countries - development of pressure tube - development of zirconium alloy	- variability in mine characteristics - time span for exposure and disease evidence - hinterland location of mines	- contracts would exhaust Ontario supply
5. Economics	- absence of industrial capability - foreign ownership - concern about coal imports	- ups and downs of uranium demands	- percentage of fuel costs to total operating costs of reactors - competitive bid for total supply impossible
6. Intergovernmental Relations	- AECL-Ontario Hydro cooperation - British and French inability to coordinate their private sector	- AECB-Ontario Mines accommodation over compliance - Failure to utilize U.S. studies	- moderate conflict over two-price system - federal supply policy - demands by Canadian allies for secure uranium supply
7. Interagency Relations	- Ontario Hydro desire not to be controlled by large private contractor	- federal split, AECB's excessive reliance on other agencies for staff support	- Ontario Hydro-Ontario Energy Ministry tension.

to the government's own interest in the nuclear industry. In the uranium contracts case, concern for a secure long-term supply (hopefully at reasonable prices) coincided with the business interests of the uranium companies and with the objective of stable employment in the mining industry.

The difference between objectives and paradigms is not always clear but the cases show that the latter are an important part of the policy climate in which intervention occurs. It is, of course, possible that paradigms are also merely more subtle rewordings of broader ideologies, albeit confined to a given policy field. The "atoms for peace" concept of the mid-1950s served to reinforce the Canadian penchant for intervention, especially since it coincided with the Pearsonian internationalism that then dominated Canadian foreign policy. In the uranium miners case one could characterize as a paradigm the regulators' opeating assumption that the mining companies bore the "front line responsibility" to propose plans for health and safety. This meant that the regulator was essentially a reactive agent in the process. This weight of reliance, or burden of proof, was in part understandable and was expressed in the context of the day-to-day responsibilities of "management." Nonetheless, it helped give substance to the otherwise less explicitly defendable "self-regulatory" ideological view which I have already noted.

The Hydro contracts case seemed at first glance to be less directly influenced by paradigms. It was affected by the emerging competition between "hard" and "soft" energy paradigms in the late 1970s, but this was rather tangential to the contracts as such. A somewhat more important factor was the growing concern in the 1970s about the "supply" side of economic management in contrast to the "demand" focus of Keynesian economics. Supply management issues were inherently less susceptible to short term "quick fixes" or incremental adjustments. This was a factor which helped the Ontario government "leap" forty years into the future to acquire secure supply at hopefully lower than world prices through the device of a long term contract.

Physical and Technological Realities: We have found it necessary to draw attention to "physical and technological realities" as a separate determinant. This will strike the lay reader of this study as being obvious. One can read many academic analyses of intervention, however, where such realities are often ignored. In the reactor program case these realities included the reactor programs of other countries and the development of pressure tube technology through zirconium alloys. In the uranium miners' case one can note the variability of mine characteristics, the sociological and spatial separation of hinterland located uranium mines from the urban located regulators, and the long timespan between exposure to radiation dust and its health effects many years later. In the Hydro case the bargaining that followed a decision to intervene was, in part, affected by the fact that the Denison and Preston contracts _together_ would, on completion, virtually exhaust Ontario's reserves of uranium. Furthermore, Hydro's position was affected by the fact that no single company could supply the contract requirements thus ruling out competitive tenders for the entire amount.

Economics: The existence of economic determinants need little elaboration. Such determinants are not entirely unrelated to the ideologies, objectives and paradigms discussed above but they deserve a separate discussion as well. For example, the reactor case study shows that the failure to adhere to the federal policy preference expressed in the mid-1950s for a large private sector involvement was influenced, in part, by the absence of industrial capability and by the existence of extensive foreign ownership. Canadian firms were relatively small and financially weak. The main branch plant firms, CGE and Westinghouse, were, in the final analysis, constrained by larger parent involvement in a competing reactor system in the United States. The uranium miners' case was also effected by the precipitous decline in the uranium market in the 1960s, a fact which made regulatory vigilance all the more unlikely. The Hydro contracts case, particularly the willingness to sign a forty year contract, was in part a product of the economic fact that uranium fuel costs are a much smaller proportion of reactor operating costs than is the case with coal or oil in conventional plants.

Intergovernmental Relations: The nature of federal-provincial and international relations also helped determine intervention objectives and outcomes. The reactor program in the 1950s was a direct product of AECL-Ontario Hydro cooperation. The predominant use of public enterprise was also based on the perceived inability of Britain and France to effectively mobilize private firms. The regulatory failure demonstrated in the uranium miners' case was, in part, a consequence of the federal-provincial conflict over inspections and compliance. Thus regulations were in place but not enforced very vigorously. It was also a product of the failure to utilize research studies from the United States as authoritative "evidence" of a hazard. In the Ontario Hydro contracts case the bargaining over the two contracts was affected by federal-Ontario conflict over a two-price versus world price policy for uranium, the pressure to acquire supply imposed on the utilities by federal uranium supply policy, the growing need for the federal and Ontario governments to accommodate each other over other broader aspects of energy and resource policy, and the demand for Canadian uranium by western allies.

Inter-Agency Relations: Finally, the nature of inter-agency relations exerts its own influence. The concern by Ontario Hydro officials in the 1950s that they would be subject to the uncertain control of a single large private contractor, a concern ultimately of their own organizational power, was stressed in the reactor case as an important factor in reversing the federal policy enunciated at the political level. The uranium miners case showed that the AECB's excessive administrative dependence on other federal (and provincial) agencies contributed to regulatory failure. Inter-agency tension between Ontario Hydro and the provincial energy ministry was also a factor in the Hydro contracts case, since the latter was a new agency attempting to exercise influence over the giant electricity utility.

Other determinants could undoubtedly be suggested in each case. For example, the relative absence of media pressure in the late 1950s and early 1960s (in an era favorable to technology) assisted the decisions to proceed with CANDU. The presence of great media pressure in the mid-1970s has undoubedly affected the pattern of intervention, particularly in drawing attention to past regulatory inadequacies.

(2) General Observations About Intervention

This description of determinants must be viewed as a summary only. There are obviously difficulties in ranking the determinants as causal factors in three case studies and in showing a strong association between particular determinants and particular instruments of intervention. It is doubtful that any totally convincing ranking or associated relationships could be presented. The case studies, for the most part, only allow us to understand policy subtleties and historical forces in the nuclear field. Nonetheless, some general observations about intervention emerge from, or are confirmed by, the analysis.

First, simple assertions that Canadian governments intervene on largely pragmatic grounds are unsatisfactory. The three cases do not show that ideology determines intervention nor that it is associated with particular instruments of intervention. Indeed, they raise interesting questions about the substitutability of instruments which I will discuss below. They do illustrate that ideology does influence the selection of interests and groups who will be the prime beneficiaries of such intervention/non-intervention decisions. Ideology can foreclose the selection of certain instruments of intervention. Equally, the three cases show that ideology is not always a sufficient determinant, but that it is a far more prevalent factor than pragmatists will admit or allow.

Second, government intervention must clearly be seen to include both overt acts of intervention and that which arises from deliberate or conscious inaction. That there are winners and losers from both kinds of intervention is obvious in the nuclear field and elsewhere. Our case studies reveal, moreover, the multiple forms and instruments through which both kinds of intervention occur. These instruments include public corporations, the use of contracts, the promulgation of regulations, the failure to ensure regulatory compliance, the funding of research, the failure to act on research results, the reorganization of agencies, and others.

Third, government intervention and actions that are in the "public interest" should not be treated as being the same thing. That intervention is in the public interest should be taken as a case to be proved or demonstrated rather than as a fact to be assumed. Those who criticize the use of public enterprise or who ideologically espouse "less" government intervention are often correct when they suggest that pro-public sector advocates want greater government involvement "on faith". In short, they equate public sector actions with the "public interest."[1] In fact, public action frequently results in the triumph of particular private or individual interests (bureaucrats, individual companies, lawyers, etc). At one level, therefore, we merely have a clash of "faiths" with no one bothering to define, or interested in defining, "public", "private", or "intervention".

A fourth, and closely related aspect of government intervention is the substitutability of governing or public policy instruments. While the analysis does not allow me to show a strong correlation between particular determinants and the use of particular instruments, it does suggest the need for policy makers to look carefully at the range of such instruments and the choice among them. Intelligent combinations of instruments may achieve better results. Hence it is essential that reformers do more than just advocate "more" regulation, "more" public enterprise or "deregulation" and "leave it to the private sector" without much thought as to the probable consequences or to the substitutability of instruments. Is there, for example, much to chose between the reactor program case where public enterprise was used, aided by moderate amounts of contracting to the private sector, and the Hydro uranium contract case, where ownership of uranium mines was foreclosed but where a 40 year contract was utilized and the uranium companies became virtually the "chosen instrument" of government. Some will argue that the first mode of intervention has resulted in a public enterprise and a heavily subsidized and non-competitive private industry. Others will point to the guaranteed profits accruing to the uranium mine owners in the second case. The point to be made here is not to deny the existence of different winners and losers in these various instruments of intervention, but to encourage a greater recognition of their possible substitutabiluty in certain circumstances and the need to analyze these carefully.

Finally, the case studies have shown that intervention cannot be divorced from perceptions of uncertainty and willingness to bear risks. Uncertainty seemed to be high in the 1950s reactor case, but risks were taken to support the technologists' claims. Uncertainty as to cause and effect relations over health hazards for miners seemed high in the 1950s, but much less so in the 1960s. In this instance regulators' actions favoured mine owners. Uncertainty over future uranium prices (and supply) was high in the third case examined but was counteracted by a long-term contract hedged by a series of risk sharing or risk averting or risk averting fall-back clauses. Intervention is obviously also affected by the perceived success or failure of previously-used alternative instruments and the degree of direct poliitical or media pressure to change the approach.

The case of the proposed selling or "privatizing" of Eldorado Nuclear Ltd., can be seen in the light of the substitution of instruments and the sharing of risk. The Clark government in 1979 intended to sell Eldorado Nuclear Ltd. (along with several other public enterprises) to symbolize and to give some substance to its belief in the need to reduce the size of government. Eldorado was to be sold, not because it was expected that its sale would change <u>nuclear</u> policy outcomes, but because it happened to be a moderately-sized company (compared to other public enterprises such as Air Canada or the CBC) which is "saleable". There were no other apparent grounds for selling Eldorado. It does, however, serve as a window on part of the uranium industry. This is a strategic consideration of some importance especially when one considers the past health and safety practices of the industry as well as the movement of multi-national oil companies into the uranium business. Moreover, it has been subsidized over the years by the federal government. Just as it is beginning to make some modest profits it was to be sold. Eldorado Nuclear has not itself been a paragon of virtue on health and safety issues, but there is no evidence whatsoever that it will behave more effectively in this respect under private auspices.

(3) Intervention and the Future of the Canadian Nuclear Industry

Government intervention in the nuclear industry has been extensive. It is fair to say that without such intervention, Canada would probably not have a nuclear industry, at least in the reactor or high technology component of the industry. In contrast to other manufacturing and resource fields, the effect of intervention has been to ensure domestic ownership of most of the industry. Largely through government auspices, an industry with high technology content and some potential for international competitiveness has been created, nurtured and sustained, albeit at very great public expense.

One could reasonably conclude that modern, international, high-technology industrial development may well be possible for countries like Canada only through the use of public enterprise and other forms of intervention. This would be a somewhat simplistic conclusion however, for the history of the Canadian nuclear industry raises quite starkly the real meaning of so-called "public" versus "private" sector involvement when, in fact, such industries must increasingly trade in political-economic markets rather than in free markets. Is a "publicly-owned" nuclear industry unique in this respect or merely a prototype of tomorrow's model? The answer to such questions often seem to rest more on ideology and belief rather than on evidence. This is not necessarily always bad since, in the face of uncertainty about future effects, one's beliefs are often as good a guide to public decisions as any other. The analysis in this volume, however, has indicated the need to examine the ways in which the instruments of public policy are or might be substituted for each other.

Another consequence of past intervention is that in the broader realm of energy policy governments have an enormous stake and vested interest in the Canadian nuclear enterprise - in nuclear energy as a future energy source. Whether this is good or bad depends greatly on one's attitude towards the economics and the safety of nuclear power in relation to other energy sources. The analysis in Chapter 5 and elsewhere has shown that some nominal pluralization of the nuclear policy process has occurred, and that therefore nuclear advocates do not go unchallenged. A large "community of interest" among federal nuclear agencies and related economic departments still exists, however. This interest is especially reinforced in the early 1980s by the attractive combination in one industry, at a time of industrial and economic decline, of both high technology and resource exports.[2] In the short and medium term future this seems likely to result in nuclear interests having disproportionate influence over energy policies. This is occurring just at a time when the Canadian situation requires the widest possible search for alternative sources of energy and a broad, judicious mix of energy policies.

It should be emphasized that nuclear energy industry officials are by no means as confident of their power as the analysis above would suggest. Indeed, they fear that they may fall victim themselves to a lack of aggressive government support for foreign reactor sales.[3] They fear that federal politicians will employ a strategy in which the nuclear technological community is kept only barely alive. The failure to secure a second CANDU sale to Argentina in 1979, a perceived split among influential ministers in the Clark and Trudeau Cabinets, a slow-down in orders by Ontario Hydro, and an unwillingness by ministers <u>to be seen</u> politically supporting nuclear development are cited as evidence of this strategy.

A further important consequence of past intervention has been the remarkable degree to which Ontario Hydro, the Ontario Government, and the Ontario taxpayer has been subsidized by the federal support of CANDU development. Future development of advanced fuel cycles and waste-management will have to insure that Ontario bears a high proportion of development and other overhead costs, especially if, as seems likely, it retains its status as Canada's primary nuclear province.[4]

The nuclear industry was born in a climate of secrecy and security. While some issues of security remain important and should not be treated lightly, there can be little doubt that the industry and its regulation must function in a far more open context than it has been accustomed to. Despite recent improvements there has been much institutional resistance to change. Not all of this resistance is to be found in bodies like the AECB and the AECL since other departments and central agencies in the nuclear policy process have been equally slow to adapt to the new demands.

Although current inadequacies are a function of institutional lag and statutory constraints, it is important to stress that problems arise from the inexperience of scientists and technologists as regulators in a regulatory climate characterized by demands for greater public involvement. The contrast in style, and operating approach between the CRTC and the AECB shows these differences quite markedly. The CRTC more willingly embraced public involvement and does not seem to fear it as has frequently been the impression left by the AECB (and to a lesser extent by other agencies).

The Nuclear Control and Administration Act (Bill C-14) presented to Parilament late in 1977 contained many reforms which would facilitate greater public involvement and a more open nuclear regulatory process. The failure to carry the Bill forward can be perceived as further evidence of political timidity and of a reluctance to accept the need for change. The fact that much of the opposition to Bill C-14 came from provincial governments has further contributed to the view that there is a total governmental reluctance to seek reform and that all the major governments, because of their own ownership or revenue stake in the nuclear and uranium industry, oppose more openness. The net effect of federal-provincial conflict, therefore, is an effective alliance against change in the nuclear policy and regulatory process.

In principle, the federal Freedom of Information bill tabled in October 1979 could have two major beneficial effects in the nuclear field.[5] It could help overcome some of the general mistrust of government evident in recent years especially if it applies to all statutes affecting nuclear matters, (e.g., the Atomic Energy Control Act, Radiation Emitting Devices Act, etc.). The potential effectiveness of such legislation is now highly dubious. Although the Atomic Energy Control Act is listed as being covered by the freedom of information legislation, there are so many exemptions listed in the bill that there would be virtually "double protection" for the secrecy of the AECB and other decision-making bodies. Exemptions such as international relations, federal-provincial relations, commercial privacy, scientific testing, and the primacy given to other statutes (including secrecy provisions of the Atomic Energy Control Act) would result, paradoxically, in even more secrecy in nuclear deliberations.

Another set of intervention choices which will tell us much about which interests will be the future winners and losers in nuclear intervention can be found in the impending decisions regarding research and development (R & D) support by government. In recent years a wide variety of areas have been suggested as being deserving of more R & D. These include research on: mine tailings; advanced fuel cycles; proliferation and safeguards characteristics of fuel cycles; long term waste disposal; low level radiation exposure; regulatory monitoring and compliance equipment; uranium supply and demand; and renewable resource technologies. In choosing among such priorities many, if not all, of the dilemmas of nuclear politics and policies emerge.[6]

There is an implicit choice between utilizing scarce R & D dollars to support <u>all</u> of these aspects of policy to a limited degree or to supporting <u>some</u> of them generously and others not at all. Since the competition for scarce R & D dollars is not confined just to nuclear or energy matters there exists also the possibility, however, remote, that there will be no new R & D resources for any of them. These R & D choices will in part at least, telegraph which interests in the nuclear debate are benefitting and those that are not. Assigning priorities is unavoidable and so will be criticism of them. If the lion's share of marginal R & D dollars and manpower goes into advanced fuel cycle work it will tell us much, for example, about the relative importance of the mine tailings question in the government's eyes.

The role of research in the policy process shows that it is often supported because decision-makers genuinely lack knowledge about a given problem or need some knowledge to keep their options open. Work on advanced fuel cycles can certainly be justified on this basis. In other instances, research can be a <u>substitute</u> for policy or a way of postponing other more concrete intervention for which lack of knowledge is not a problem. Growing government intervention in the nuclear industry in the future seems to be a virtual certainty. Conflicting views about Canada's nuclear future and whether we should have one, are profound and deeply held. They are embedded in growing concern about the proper social management of technology. In a democracy, they deserve the widest possible public evaluation and discussion.

Whether one is exploring future R & D funding, regulatory reform, or even the selling of Eldorado Nuclear Ltd. as manifestations of "intervention", it is hoped that the analysis in this volume has shed light on the complexities of government intervention. It is hoped that the study has also shown the need for a frank appraisal of the use of various modes of intervention, including designed inaction, and of the modern meaning of public sector-private sector relations in industrial development and nuclear policy in Canada.

NOTES: CHAPTER 9

1. Some of the many and conflicting definitions of the public interest can be found in W.T. Stanbury, "Definitions of the 'Public Interest'," Appendix D in Douglas G. Hartle, Public Policy Decision Making and Regulation (Montreal: Institute for Research on Public Policy, 1979), pp. 213-218.

2. For data on uranium exports, see Leonard and Partners Ltd., Economic Impact of Nuclear Energy Industry in Canada. Detail Report. (Ottawa: Leonnard and Partners, 1978) p. F-1.

3. J.M. Douglas, A Report By the Task Force On CANDU Export Marketing (Ottawa: 1979).

4. See G. Bruce Doern and Gordon Sims, "Atomic Energy of Canada Ltd." in G. Bruce Doern ed. Spending Tax Dollars: Federal Expenditures 1980-81 (Ottawa: School of Public Administration, Carleton University, 1980).

5. President of Privy Council, Freedom of Information Legislation: Discussion Paper (Ottawa: October 1979).

6. See Science Council of Canada, Roads to Energy Self-Reliance (Ottawa: Minister of Supply and Services Canada, 1979).

– 199 –

Appendix A

The nuclear fuel cycle

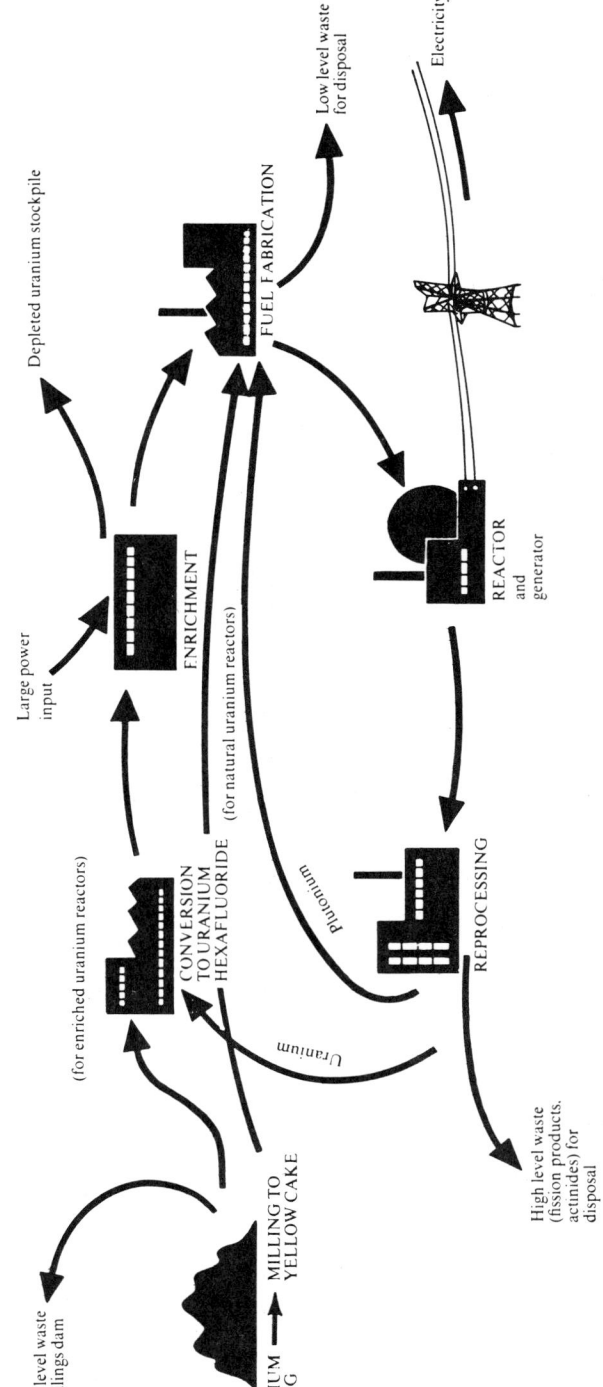

Source: *Ranger Uranium Environmental Inquiry, First Report* (Canberra: Australian Government Publishing Service, 1976), p. 22.

Appendix B

MAIN PROVISIONS OF DENISON CONTRACT

ATTRIBUTE	DENISON CONTRACT
1. Essential Elements	
1.1 Quantity	126 million lbs
1.2 Initial Capital Cost funded by Hydro (1975$)	$151 million (+ escalation) (The $25 million advanced on signing the contract)
1.3 Pricing Formula	Base + 1/2 (World-Base) but no lower than Base
1.4 Base Price	Operating Costs + Depreciation + Mining Taxes + $5/lb (escalated) + $0.50/lb ----------------
1.5 Annual Deliveries	up to 1 Million lbs 1980-1983 2 Million lbs 1984-1993 6 Million lbs 1994-2010 2 Million lbs 2011
1.6 Repayment of Advances	1/30 per year for 30 years
1.7 Dedication of Reserve	81.5 Million lbs already contracted 126 Million lbs for Hydro only Any further reserves can be sold to others, subject to Hydro approval.
1.8 Premature Termination Provisions	1. Force Majeure for 5 years (on either party) 2. Economic Obsolescence after 1985 (Base Exceeds World Price for five years)
1.9 Most Favoured Supplier	Increase Price to match price/margin received by another Elliot Lake producer
1.10 Sellers Facilities	Mine & Mill capable of meeting 50% of required contractual production are in existence
1.11 Provisions of Further Facilities	Hydro pays only for initial expansion
2. Security Elements	
2.1 Security for Advances	Subordinated Mortgage on Elliot Lake Mine and Reserves.
2.2 Prior Encumbrance	$100 Million 1976 to $300 Million 1981
2.3 Exposure to Financial Risk	Involved in Other Corporate Activities.
2.4 Termination for Economic Obsolescence	Hydro Forfeits unrepaid Advances
2.5 Termination by Producer under Force Majeure	Repayment of Advances prorated if production exceeds 50% capacity.

Appendix B (continued)

ATTRIBUTE	DENISON CONTRACT
3. **Reliability of Estimates**	
3.1 Annual Production Rates	6 million lbs/year appears reasonable to 1999, when further expansion may be required.
3.2 Construction Costs	Estimated based on preliminary mining plan, prepared by mine staff but reviewed by Hydro consultants.
3.3 Ore Reserves	Considered Reliable
4. **Sale of Surplus**	
4.1 Sole agent	Sole Agent for Denison Concentrates
4.2 Profits	Split 50/50 after costs
4.3 Time Limit	Hydro has right to sell after 18 months
5. **Quantity Variations**	
5.1 Recourse for Oversupply	1. Sell Excess 2. Order Curtailment and reimburse Denison up to $5/lb for quantity curtailed - only if export sales prohibited. (Up to 5 curtailment of 5% each).
5.2 Inability of Hydro to use the uranium due to Force Majeure	Excused from taking delivery
5.3 Assurance of supply and reduction by producer	Up to 10% allowable in any year below this level (chronically) default (ex force majeure).
6. **Financial Terms**	
6.1 Provision of Capital	Hydro funds Expansion Project Sustaining Capital and further Expansion funded by Denison.
6.2 Initial Capital Cost/lb (1975 $'s)	$1.20/lb
6.3 Working Capital	Supplied by Denison
6.4 Operating Cost/lb (1975 $'s)	$15.54 (starting 1980).

* Source: Summary provided by the staff of the Ontario Select Committee on Ontario Hydro (Toronto, 1978).

Appendix C

MAIN PROVISIONS OF PRESTON CONTRACT

	ATTRIBUTE	PRESTON CONTRACT
1.	**Essential Elements**	
1.1	Quantity	Up to entire reserve, estimated at 72 million lbs.
1.2	Initial Capital Cost funded by Hydro (1975$)	$188 million (+ escalation) advanced as required.
1.3	Pricing Formula	Base + 1/3 (World-Base) but no lower than Base.
1.4	Base Price	Operating Costs + Depreciation + Mining Taxes + $5/lb (escalated) ----------- (+ Capital Taxes)
1.5	Annual Deliveries	2.0 million lbs 1984-2020 Option to double capacity
1.6	Repayment of Advances	Cashflow (without income tax deducted) less $5/lb (escalated) but in no shorter period than 14 years.
1.7	Dedication of Reserve	Full 72 million lbs and any increase dedicated to Hydro
1.8	Premature Termination Provisions	1. Escalation of Capital or Operating Costs after definitive study 2. Low production (actual or forecast) for 3 consecutive years 3. Optional Termination by Hydro with Forfeiture of Unrepaid Advances 4. Force Majeure for 4 years (on either party)
1.9	Most Favoured Supplier	No clause but a fair contract expected
1.10	Sellers Facilities	No production capability presently exists
1.11	Provisions of Further Facilities	Hydro supplies all capital requirements (initial and ongoing)
2.	**Security Elements**	
2.1	Security for Advances	Mortgage on Mine and Reserves
2.2	Prior Encumbrance	No Prior nor pari-passu Encumbrance until indebtedness to Hydro reaches zero.
2.3	Exposure to Financial Risk	Only other interest is share holding in Rio Algom.
2.4	Termination for Economic Obsolescence	Hydro Forfeits unrepaid Advances
2.5	Termination by Producer under Force Majeure	Hydro & Preston share cash flow from continued operation or sale of assets.

Appendix C (continued)

ATTRIBUTE	PRESTON CONTRACT
3. **Reliability of Estimates**	
3.1 Annual Production Rates	2.0 million lbs/ year appears reasonable for at least 20 years. Expansion up to 4 million lbs/year appears feasible.
3.2 Construction Cost	Feasibility Study prepared by an independent firm of Mining Consultants. Reviewed by Hydro consultants.
3.3 Ore Reserves	Considered Reliable. Full extent of reserves not totally delineated.
4. **Sale of Surplus**	
4.1 Sole Agent	Sole Agent for Preston Concentrates
4.2 Profits	Split 50/50 after costs
4.3 Time Limit	Hydro has right to sell after 9 months
5. **Quantity Variations**	
5.1 Recourse for Oversupply	1. Sell excess 2. Cutback production up to 15% on 1 year's notice, for a period of at least 3 years. 3. Terminate contract on 5 years' notice forfeiting unrepaid advances.
5.2 Inability of Hydro to use the Uranium due to Force Majeure	Excused from taking delivery.
5.3 Assurance of Supply and Reduction by Producer	No reduction by Producer permitted. Best efforts for full supply with default below average of 85% (ex force majeure)
6. **Financial Terms**	
6.1 Provision of Capital	Hydro pays all Capital Costs including Option for expansion
6.2 Initial Capital Cost/lb (1975 $'s)	$2.62/lb (for 2 million lbs/year)
6.3 Working Capital	Supplied by Hydro
6.4 Operating Cost/lb (1975 $'s)	$16.75 (starting 1984)

* Source: Summary provided by the staff of the Ontario Select Committee on Hydro Hydro (Toronto, 1978).

The Institute for Research on Public Policy
PUBLICATIONS AVAILABLE*
March, 1980

BOOKS

Leroy O. Stone & Claude Marceau	*Canadian Population Trends and Public Policy Through the 1980's.* 1977 $4.00
Raymond Breton	*The Canadian Condition: A Guide to Research in Public Policy.* 1977 (No Charge)
Raymond Breton	*Une orientation de la recherche politique dans le contexte canadien.* 1978 (No Charge)
J.W. Rowley & W.T. Stanbury, eds.	*Competition Policy in Canada: Stage II, Bill C-13.* 1978 $12.95
C.F. Smart & W.T. Stanbury, eds.	*Studies on Crisis Management.* 1978 $9.95
W.T. Stanbury, ed.	*Studies on Regulation in Canada.* 1978 $9.95
Michael Hudson	*Canada in the New Monetary Order—Borrow? Devalue? Restructure!* 1978 $6.95
W.A.W. Neilson & J.C. MacPherson, eds.	*The Legislative Process in Canada: The Need for Reform.* 1978 $12.95
David K. Foot, ed.	*Public Employment and Compensation in Canada: Myths and Realities.* 1978 $10.95
W.E. Cundiff & Mado Reid, eds.	*Issues in Canada/U.S. Transborder Computer Data Flows.* 1979 $6.50
G.B. Reschenthaler & B. Roberts, eds.	*Perspectives on Canadian Airline Regulation.* 1979 $13.50
P.K. Gorecki & W.T. Stanbury, eds.	*Perspectives on the Royal Commission on Corporate Concentration.* 1979 $15.95
David K. Foot	*Public Employment in Canada: A Statistical Series.* 1979 $15.00

---

* Order Address: The Institute for Research on Public Policy
P.O. Box 9300, Station "A"
TORONTO, Ontario
M5W 2C7

Meyer W. Bucovetsky, ed.	*Studies on Public Employment and Compensation.* 1979 $14.95
Richard French & André Béliveau	*The RCMP and the Management of National Security.* 1979 $6.95
Richard French & André Béliveau	*La GRC et la Gestion de la Sécurité nationale.* 1979 $7.95
Leroy O. Stone & Michael J. MacLean	*Future Income Prospects for Canada's Senior Citizens.* 1979 $7.95
Douglas G. Hartle	*Public Policy Decision Making and Regulation.* 1979 $12.95
Richard Bird (in collaboration with Bucovetsky & Foot)	*The Growth of Public Employment in Canada.* 1979 $12.95
G. Bruce Doern & Allan M. Maslove, eds.	*The Public Evaluation of Government Spending.* 1979 $10.95
Richard Price, ed.	*The Spirit of the Alberta Indian Treaties.* 1979 $8.95
Peter N. Nemetz, ed.	*Energy Policy: The Global Challenge.* 1979 $16.95
Richard J. Schultz	*Federalism and the Regulatory Process.* 1979 $1.50
Lionel D. Feldman & Katherine A. Graham	*Bargaining for Cities, Municipalities and Intergovernmental Relations: An Assessment.* 1979 $10.95
Elliot J. Feldman & Neil Nevitte, eds.	*The Future of North America: Canada, the United States, and Quebec Nationalism.* 1979 $7.95
Maximo Halty-Carrere	*Technological Development Strategies for Developing Countries.* 1979 $12.95
G.B. Reschenthaler	*Occupational Health and Safety in Canada: The Economics and Three Case Studies.* 1979 $5.00
David R. Protheroe	*Imports and Politics: Trade Decision-Making in Canada, 1968-1979.* 1980 $8.95
G. Bruce Doern	*Government Intervention in the Canadian Nuclear Industry.* 1980 $8.95

G. Bruce Doern & R.W. Morrison, eds.	*Canadian Nuclear Policies.* 1980
W.T. Stanbury, ed.	*Government Regulation: Scope, Growth, Process.* 1980.

OCCASIONAL PAPERS ($3.00 per copy)

W.E. Cundiff (No. 1)	*Nodule Stock? Seabed Mining and the Future of the Canadian Nickel Industry.* 1978
IRPP/Brookings (No. 2)	*Conference on Canadian-U.S. Economic Relations.* 1978
Robert A. Russell (No. 3)	*The Electronic Briefcase: The Office of the Future.* 1978
C.C. Gotlieb (No. 4)	*Computers in the Home.* 1978
Raymond Breton & Gail Grant Akian (No. 5)	*Urban Institutions and People of Indian Ancestry.* 1978
K.A. Hay (No. 6)	*Friends or Acquaintances? Canada as a Resource Supplier to the Japanese Economy.* 1978
T. Atkinson (No. 7)	*Trends in Life Satisfaction.* 1979
M. McLean (No. 8)	*The Impact of the Micro-electronics Industry on the Structure of the Canadian Economy.* 1979
Fred Thompson & W.T. Stanbury (No. 9)	*The Political Economy of Interest Groups in the Legislative Process in Canada.* 1979
Gordon B. Thompson (No. 10)	*Memo from Mercury: Information Technology is Different.* 1979
Pierre Sormany (No. 11)	*Les Micro-Esclaves Vers Une Bio-Industrie Canadienne.* 1979
K. Hartley, P.N. Nemetz, S. Schwartz, D. Uyeno, I. Vertinsky & J. Young (No. 12)	*Energy R & D Decision Making for Canada.* 1979.

WORKING PAPERS (No Charge)**

W.E. Cundiff (No. 1) — *Issues in Canada/U.S. Transborder Computer Data Flows.* 1978 (Out of print; in IRPP book of same title.)

John Cornwall (No. 2) — *Industrial Investment and Canadian Economic Growth: Some Scenarios for the Eighties.* 1978

Russell Wilkins — *L'éspérance de vie par quartier à Montréal, 1976: un indicateur social pour la planification.* 1979

** Order Working Papers from
The Institute for Research on Public Policy
P.O. Box 3670
Halifax South
Halifax, Nova Scotia
B3J 3K6